# *T*esla's Bioenergetic Blueprint: Healing the Human Field Through Frequency, Mapping & Coherence

Dr. Constance Santego
Maximillian Enterprises
Kelowna, BC

Copy Editor & Interior Design: Dr. Constance Santego
Book Layout: ©2017 BookDesignTemplates.com
Ordering Information:
Quantity sales. Special discounts are available on quantity purchases
by corporations, associations, and others. For details, contact the
email below (addressed: "Special Sales Department").

Trade Paperback ISBN: 978-1-997907-12-1
eBook ISBN: 978-1-997907-13-8
Created and published In Canada. Printed and bound in the
United States of America

First Edition
Published by Maximillian Enterprises
Kelowna, BC
Canada

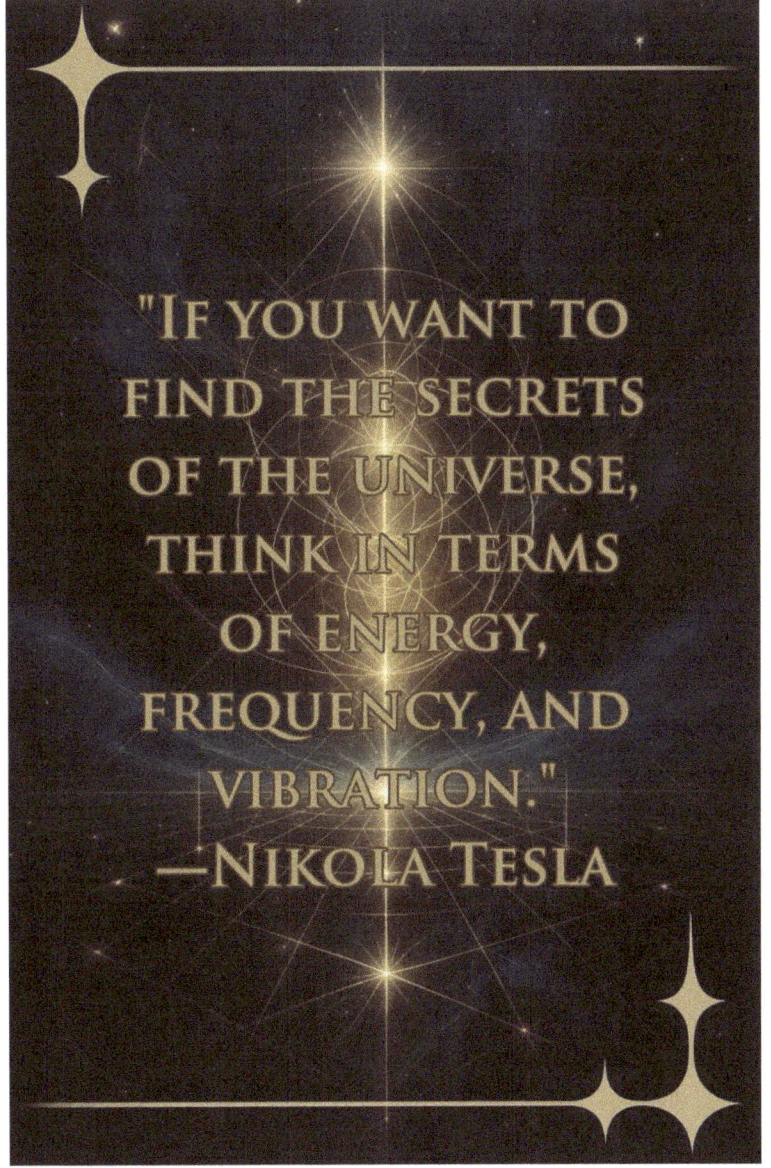

"IF YOU WANT TO FIND THE SECRETS OF THE UNIVERSE, THINK IN TERMS OF ENERGY, FREQUENCY, AND VIBRATION."
—NIKOLA TESLA

*D*edicated to the pioneers of

frequency, light, and vibration—
To Nikola Tesla, whose vision
electrified the world and illuminated
unseen realms of energy,
And to every soul courageous enough
to listen to the whispers of the unseen,
to heal beyond the veil of matter, and
bring light where others see darkness.

This book is for you—
The future healers, the bridge-
builders,
the ones who remember that spirit
and science are not opposites,
but companions in our evolution.

May this work ignite the spark within
you.

## ALSO BY DR. CONSTANCE SANTEGO

**NOVELS**
Illegitimate Grace
Ashcroft Hollow

**Okanagan Trilogy:**
Beneath the Vineyards
Under the Okanagan Sun
Guardian of the Lake

**The Nine Spiritual Gifts Series:**
Journey of a Soul – (Vol 1 Michael)
Language of a Soul – (Vol 2 Gabriel)
Prophecy of a Soul – (Vol 3 Bath Kol)
Healing of a Soul – (Vol 4 Raphael)
Miracles of a Soul – (Vol 5 Hamied)
Knowledge of a Soul – (Vol 6 Raziel)
Wisdom of a Soul – (Vol 7 Uriel)
Faith of a Soul – (Vol 8 Pistis Sophia)

**NONFICTION**
The Intuitive Life, The Gift Of Prophecy, Third Edition
Fairy Tales, Dreams And Reality… *Where Are You On Your Path?*
*Second Edition*
Your Persona… The Mask You Wear
Archangel Michael's Soul Retrieval Guide
Bend, Don't Break: *Finding Your Way Back To Abundance*
Ring Therapy: *A Guide To Healing And Balance*
Ring Therapy Pocket Guide
Beyond The Mind: *Harnessing The Power Of Astral Projection For Creative*
*Awakening*
Floraopathy™: *The Art And Science Of Vibrational Healing With*
*Essential Oils*
Dear Older Me: A Memoir… *Of Sorts*
It's Just Like Poker: *A Spiritual Guide To Playing The*
*Cards Life Deals You*
Signs And Meanings: *What The Feet Reveal About Health, Stress, And*
*The Body's Story*
Auricions: *Unlocking Subconscious Healing Through Quantum Medicine*
Quick Fix Acupressure Method
Manifestation – *The DREAM Method in 5 Steps*
Confidence – *Mastering the Dream Method*
The New Paradigm: *Conscious Healing In The Age Of Ai*

**TESLA SERIES:**
Tesla And The Future Of Energy Medicine
Beyond Tesla: *Advancing The Science Of Energy Healing*
Tesla's Code: *Mastering Energy, Frequency, And Creative Power*

**REIKI WISDOM, SERIES:**
Angelic Lifestyle, a Vibrant Lifestyle
Angelic Lifestyle 42-Day Energy Cleanse
Reiki and the Power of The Joint Points: Unlocking Energy Pathways
for Healing (Vol I)
Reiki and Karmic Healing: *Releasing Patterns From Past Lives* (Vol II)
Reiki and the Five Elements (Vol III)
Secrets of a Healer, Magic Of Reiki
The Reiki Master's Manual *(In English, German, Spanish, French, Portuguese, Russian, Hindi, and Mandarin Chinese)*

**CHAKRA SERIES:**
Heart Chakra 101: The Bridge
Root Chakra 101: Building Safety, Survival, Foundation
Sacral Chakra 101: Creativity, Pleasure, Emotions
Solar Plexus Chakra 101: Power, Confidence, Will
Throat Chakra 101: Truth, Voice, Self-Expression
Third Eye Chakra 101: Intuition, Vision, Insight
Crown Chakra 101: Spiritual Connection, Transcendence.

**SECRETS OF A HEALER, SERIES:**
Magic Of Aromatherapy (Vol I)
Magic Of Reflexology (Vol II)
Magic Of The Gifts (Vol III)
Magic Of Muscle Testing (Vol IV)
Magic Of Iridology (Vol V)
Magic Of Massage (Vol VI)
Magic Of Hypnotherapy (Vol VII)
Magic Of Reiki (Vol VIII)
Magic Of Advanced Aromatherapy (Vol IX)
Magic Of Esthetics (Vol X)
The Reiki Master's Manual (Vol XI)

**ADULT COLORING JOURNALS**
SERIES-ZEN COLORING:
Quantum Energy and Mindful Living Journal (Vol 1)
Reiki Energy Journal (Vol 2)
Nine Spiritual Gifts Journal (Vol 3)
I Forgive Journal (Vol 4)

**FOR CHILDREN**
I am Big Tonight. I Don't Need the Light
The Magic Elf Book: 25 Days of Surprises

**COOKBOOK**
My Favorite Recipes, with a Hint of Giggle

**BUISNESS**
How To Use ChatGPT For Authors: From Idea To Published Book
Scaling Beyond 6 Figures: Strategies For Health & Wellness
Professionals
The Academypreneur's Playbook: Turn Knowledge Into A
Revenue-Generating School

**HUMOR/GIFT BOOK**
How Do You Like Your Eggs? *Crack Into Your Personality, Yolk and All*

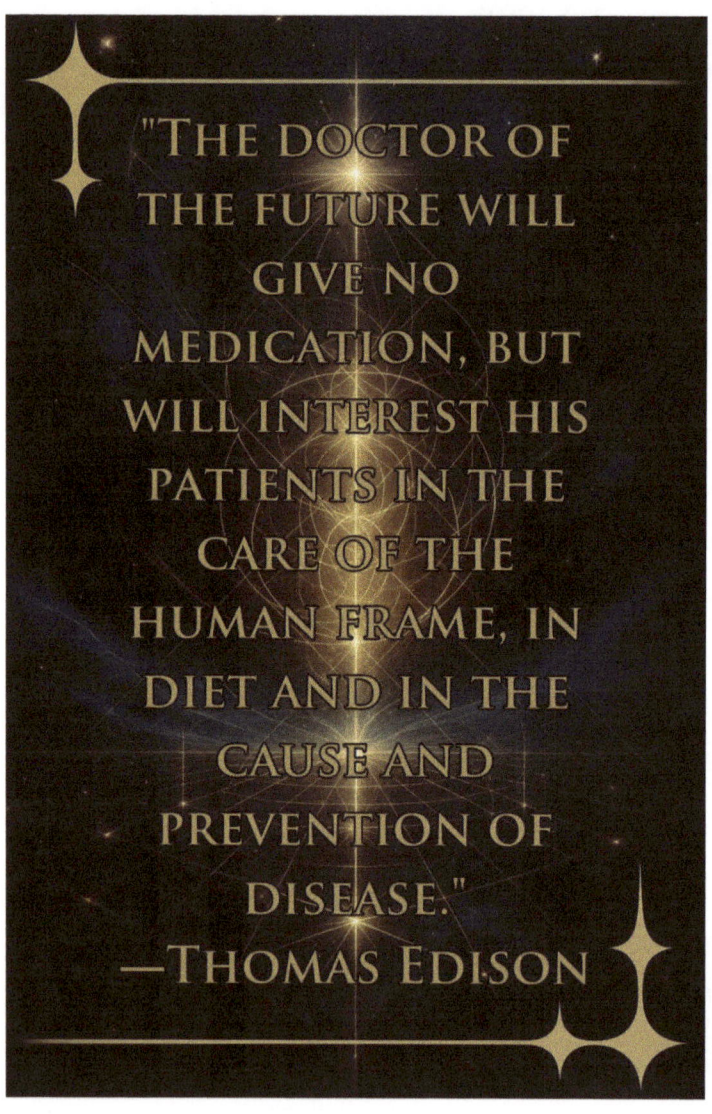

"THE DOCTOR OF THE FUTURE WILL GIVE NO MEDICATION, BUT WILL INTEREST HIS PATIENTS IN THE CARE OF THE HUMAN FRAME, IN DIET AND IN THE CAUSE AND PREVENTION OF DISEASE."
—THOMAS EDISON

# Contents

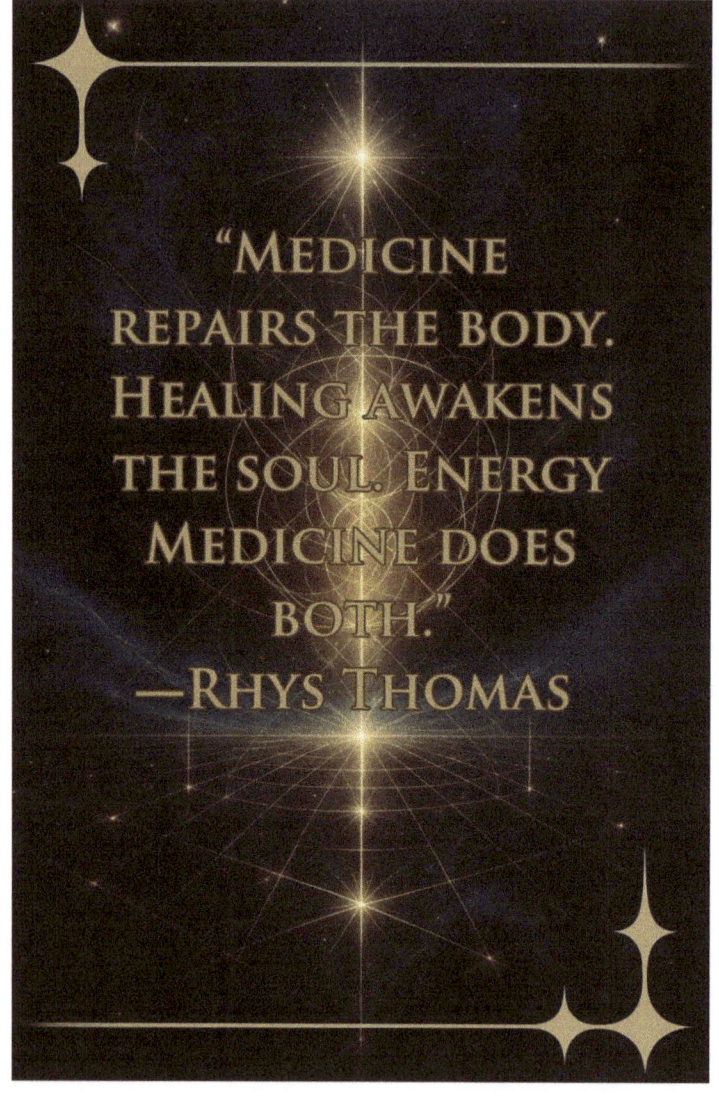

"MEDICINE REPAIRS THE BODY. HEALING AWAKENS THE SOUL. ENERGY MEDICINE DOES BOTH."
—RHYS THOMAS

# Foreword

*I*n an age where science races ahead and the human soul yearns for deeper meaning, we find ourselves at a crossroads—a moment where ancient wisdom and futuristic innovation must meet in harmony. Nikola Tesla, a pioneer of invisible forces, understood that the universe speaks in the language of frequency, vibration, and energy. While history remembers him for electricity, those who look deeper see a man who envisioned healing technologies that operated beyond wires and machines— he saw into the field of life itself.

*Tesla's Bioenergetic Blueprint* is more than a book. It is a bridge between what is known and what is felt. It awakens the silent truths hidden in our cells, in the aether, in the forgotten codes of natural intelligence. It challenges us to reframe healing—not as something we receive, but as something we activate from within.

In these pages, you will be guided through the principles of bioenergetic healing inspired by Tesla's lesser-known work. You'll uncover not only scientific insights but practical protocols, case studies, and energetic truths that transcend the limitations of conventional medicine. This is the sacred territory of the energy body, the quantum field, and the awakened healer.

Whether you are a practitioner, a seeker, or a curious soul walking your own path of evolution, this book will speak to the frequency of your spirit. You are not just reading Tesla's legacy—you are living it.

Let this be your blueprint.

"EVERYTHING IN LIFE IS VIBRATION."
—ALBERT EINSTEIN

# Preface

## *A* Continuum of Energy, Evolution, and Empowerment

When I began writing *Tesla and the Future of Energy Medicine*, I set out to explore the forgotten genius of Nikola Tesla—not just the inventor, but the visionary who understood that energy, frequency, and vibration were the very keys to health, consciousness, and the future of healing. That first book opened the gateway. It laid the philosophical and historical foundation, igniting curiosity and attracting healers, researchers, and readers ready to step beyond conventional paradigms.

The second book, *Beyond Tesla: Advancing the Science of Energy Healing*, took the leap forward. In it, I explored the technologies, innovations, and global healing practices that continue to build on Tesla's legacy—connecting the dots between subtle energy, biofield science, and cutting-edge vibrational medicine. This volume invited readers to reimagine what's possible, not just in theory, but in practice.

Then came *Tesla's Code: Mastering Energy, Frequency & Creative Power*. This third installment turned inward. It was not just about healing others—but about awakening the inner Tesla within each of us. I introduced creative visualization, frequency mastery, and the vibrational power of thought, belief, and spiritual energy. This book became a bridge between science and soul.

## Why This Fourth Book?

Now, with *Tesla's Bioenergetic Blueprint*, I offer the missing link: a system for **mapping the human energy field**, decoding emotional imprints, and applying Tesla-inspired frequency healing through the lens of **bioenergetics**.

This book brings the previous three volumes full circle—integrating:

- The historical roots of Tesla's discoveries (*Book 1*),
- The expanding field of modern frequency healing (*Book 2*),
- The individual's inner power to heal and create (*Book 3*),

—into a **practitioner-level model** that can be used in clinics, healing sessions, personal practice, and professional training.

You'll discover tools, methods, and protocols grounded in:

- Touch-based energetic reading
- Frequency pairings and coherence fields
- Biofield mapping and emotional release
- Conscious intention, breath, and intuitive sensing
- Tesla's core principles applied through modern energetic frameworks

# Who This Book Is For

This book is written for those who are ready to move from theory to **embodied mastery**—energy healers, holistic practitioners, intuitive therapists, and even curious scientists who believe the body is more than biology.

You do not need to be a physicist or a mystic to use this work. You need only an open mind, willing hands, and a sincere desire to heal.

If the first three books lit your path, this one gives you the **compass, coordinates, and coherence tools** to walk it.

Welcome to the next evolution of Tesla-inspired healing. Welcome to *The Bioenergetic Blueprint*.

— *Dr. Constance Santego, Ph.D., DNM*

# Note to Reader

Dear Reader,

If you've journeyed through the first three books in the Tesla healing series—

- *Tesla and the Future of Energy Medicine,*
- *Beyond Tesla: Advancing the Science of Energy Healing,* and
- *Tesla's Code: Mastering Energy Frequency and Creative Power*—
  you already know the profound power of frequency, vibration, and the human biofield.

Each of those volumes revealed a different facet of Tesla's energetic legacy. From exploring disruptive healing technologies to decoding frequency as a universal intelligence, we've traveled through science, intuition, and innovation.

This fourth book, *Tesla's Bioenergetic Blueprint*, picks up the thread—and grounds it.

Here, we bridge high-frequency theory with hands-on application. This book introduces **Energeneics**, a next-generation system for mapping, reading, and restoring the human energy field. It draws from bioenergetics, coherence science, frequency medicine, and Tesla's visionary principles to bring energy healing down to the cellular and emotional level.

You'll discover how to:

- Tune the human field using sound, scent, light, and subtle sensing.
- Read emotional blocks through muscle testing and frequency feedback.
- Create deep healing shifts using the Energeneic Mapping system™.
- Understand how Tesla's legacy of resonance, coherence, and energy transmission continues to evolve today.

Whether you're a healer, seeker, or skeptic, this book is your invitation to enter the next evolution of energy medicine—not just as an idea, but as a practice you can experience in your own hands.

Welcome to the future of healing.
It begins in your biofield.
It resonates through your intention.
And it is encoded, always, in frequency.

# Learning Outcome

*B*y the end of this book, readers will be able to:

**Understand the Foundations of Tesla-Inspired Bioenergetics**
Gain a clear understanding of Nikola Tesla's core energy principles—frequency, vibration, and resonance—and how they relate to modern concepts in energy medicine and the human biofield.

**Explore the Human Energy Field as a Living Blueprint**
Recognize the structure and function of the subtle energy systems (auric layers, chakras, meridians) and how they interact with emotional, physical, and spiritual health.

**Learn to Map Energetic Imbalances Using the Energeneic Method**
Discover how to detect, interpret, and shift energetic disruptions using advanced mapping techniques rooted in bioenergetics, muscle testing, and frequency sensitivity.

### Apply Frequency-Based Interventions for Self-Healing

Gain practical tools to harmonize the body's field using sound, light, breath, intention, sacred geometry, and Tesla-inspired frequencies.

### Cultivate Intuition as a Diagnostic and Healing Tool

Train your subtle sensing and intuitive faculties to work in concert with energetic anatomy, supporting more accurate readings and deeply transformational healing.

### Develop Personal Coherence and Inner Resonance

Learn coherence techniques to align heart-brain states, raise your vibratory rate, and stabilize the nervous system—laying the foundation for intuitive insight and health restoration.

### Bridge Science and Spirit through Bioenergetic Consciousness

Build a cohesive understanding that blends ancient energy practices, modern quantum biology, and Tesla's visionary principles into a unified healing paradigm.

# Tesla's Bioenergetic Blueprint: Healing the Human Field Through Frequency, Mapping & Coherence

Dr. Constance Santego

# PART I — THEORETICAL FOUNDATIONS

# Chapter 1: Tesla's Legacy in Human Energy Understanding

*N*ikola Tesla once said, *"If you want to find the secrets of the universe, think in terms of energy, frequency, and vibration."*
These words, often quoted but rarely understood in their full depth, form the foundation of a revolution—a new way of understanding the human being not as merely biological, but as fundamentally energetic.

This book, *Tesla's Bioenergetic Blueprint: Healing the Human Field Through Frequency, Mapping & Coherence*, builds upon Tesla's forgotten visions, weaving them together with modern discoveries in vibrational medicine, frequency-based healing, and the emerging science of the biofield.

**Tesla's Vision Beyond Electricity**

To the public, Tesla is known as the father of alternating current, wireless power, and radio waves. But his deeper obsession was far more esoteric: the resonance between all living things. He believed that energy could be harnessed not only to power machines, but also to restore balance to the human body and mind.

In his Colorado Springs experiments, Tesla noted that the earth itself had a natural frequency. He imagined a world where people could tap into these planetary harmonics for healing—where human beings could be aligned like tuning forks, resonating in harmony with the cosmos.

## Vibrational Medicine and the Biofield

Modern science is finally catching up to Tesla's intuitions. Researchers now describe the human biofield as an organizing field of energy and information that envelops and permeates the body. When this field is coherent— meaning it is stable, harmonious, and aligned—health flourishes. When it is disrupted, symptoms begin to manifest on physical, emotional, and mental levels.

Tesla's language of frequency and vibration matches perfectly with today's concepts:

- **Resonance**: When two systems vibrate at the same frequency, energy transfer becomes effortless.
- **Coherence**: The synchronization of waveforms leads to biological efficiency and mental clarity.
- **Phase and Amplitude**: Describe not just radio signals, but also the language of the heart, brainwaves, and even the chakras.

## The Human Energy System Through Tesla's Lens

This book proposes a bold integration: that Tesla's framework of oscillating systems, scalar waves, and field harmonics applies directly to the structure of the human energetic system. We'll explore:

- How Tesla's scalar energy theories explain long-distance healing
- Why coherence between the heart and brain mirrors Tesla's concept of *sympathetic resonance*
- How the chakra system might be seen as vibratory nodes in a larger harmonic blueprint

- The idea that energy mapping protocols (like The Energeneic Blueprint™) are a continuation of Tesla's belief in patterned energy intelligence

## From Technology to Inner Technology

Tesla foresaw a future where "the day science begins to study non-physical phenomena, it will make more progress in one decade than in all the previous centuries of its existence." This book answers that call—not just through external devices, but by revealing **inner technologies**: the breath, the mind, intention, sound, color, and mapping systems that realign the biofield.

We do not need to plug into machines to be healed—we are the instruments. The human body, when properly attuned, is a Tesla coil of healing energy.

## Bridging the Past and the Future

This is not just another Tesla book, nor just another bioenergetics manual. This is the convergence.
*Tesla's Code* taught us to awaken our creative power.
*Beyond Tesla* advanced the science of frequency-based healing.
Now, *Tesla's Bioenergetic Blueprint* will give readers the tools to **map**, **measure**, and **realign** their human energy systems—merging ancient intuitive systems with Tesla's futuristic insights, and grounding them in practical healing tools.

Welcome to the Blueprint.

## Mini Tesla Timeline: From Electricity to Energy Healing

| Year | Milestone |
|---|---|
| 1884 | Tesla arrives in New York, begins working for Edison. |
| 1888 | Develops and patents the **Alternating Current (AC)** system. |
| 1891 | Invents the **Tesla Coil**, exploring high-voltage energy transmission. |
| 1899 | **Colorado Springs Experiments**: Studies Earth resonance & Schumann waves. |
| 1901–1905 | Builds **Wardenclyffe Tower**, aiming to transmit wireless energy globally. |
| 1910s–1920s | Focus shifts to **non-physical energy**, scalar fields, resonance theory. |
| Late Life | Writes on the **vibrational nature of health**, energy, and the cosmos. |

*"The day science begins to study non-physical phenomena, it will make more progress in one decade than in all the previous centuries of its existence." — Nikola Tesla*

# Quick Look: The 3 Pillars of Tesla Healing

"If you want to find the secrets of the universe, think in terms of **energy, frequency, and vibration**." — Nikola Tesla

Tesla's model isn't just for machines—it applies directly to the human energy field. Here's how:

 **FREQUENCY**

**What we emit.**
Every organ, emotion, and thought has a frequency. This is your body's broadcast—an energetic signal that shapes your health, mood, and even relationships. *Example:* A calm person emits a different brainwave frequency than someone under stress.

 **VIBRATION**

**How we feel.**
This is your internal state—your "vibe." High vibration states like love, joy, and gratitude lead to vitality. Low vibrations like fear and anger lead to disharmony. *Example:* Gratitude has a measurable high-heart coherence frequency, while resentment disrupts that flow.

RESONANCE

**How we align.**
Resonance is about connection. When you match frequencies with another person, place, or healing tool, energy flows effortlessly between you. *Example:* Standing barefoot on the Earth (Earthing) can synchronize your body with the Earth's 7.83 Hz Schumann frequency.

# What Is Bioenergetics?

**Bioenergetics** is the study and practice of how **energy flows through living systems**—especially the human body—and how that energy can be measured, balanced, and optimized to promote physical, emotional, and spiritual well-being.

At its core, bioenergetics recognizes that the human body is not just a physical structure, but an **electromagnetic field of living information**. Every thought, emotion, movement, and organ function generates or is influenced by bioelectrical signals, frequencies, and subtle energies.

Imagine your body is like a phone. Just like a phone needs a battery and electrical signals to work, your body also uses energy to power everything you do—thinking, moving, healing, even feeling emotions. Bioenergetics looks at **how that energy is created, moved, blocked, or balanced** inside you.

This energy isn't just calories from food—it's also the **subtle energy** that some cultures call **chi, prana, or life force.** Bioenergetics blends science and tradition to understand how this invisible energy field affects your health.

In *Tesla's Bioenergetic Blueprint*, this field is explored not only through ancient systems like chakras and meridians, but also through **Tesla's lens of vibration, frequency, and resonance**—blending spiritual science with cutting-edge energy medicine.

## A Brief History of Bioenergetics

Bioenergetics has roots in **both ancient wisdom** and **modern science**:

- **Ancient Roots**: Thousands of years ago, cultures in China, India, and Egypt already believed in life force energy. They used practices like **acupuncture, yoga, and Reiki** to move and balance this energy.
- **Mid-1900s**: A psychiatrist named **Wilhelm Reich** believed that emotions were stored in the body and that energy could get "stuck," leading to illness. He inspired body-based therapies that tried to release emotional blocks.
- **1970s–80s**: Scientists like **Dr. Alexander Lowen** and others developed **bioenergetic therapy**, a method that uses breath, movement, and bodywork to help people release emotional tension.
- **Modern Day**: Today, bioenergetics includes the study of the **human biofield** (an invisible field of energy that surrounds the body), **frequency medicine**, **muscle testing**, and even technologies like **pulsed magnetic therapy** or **light therapy**.

## What Bioenergetics Is Not (Especially Not Biogenetics)

It's easy to confuse *bioenergetics* with *biogenetics*, but they are totally different!

| Term | What It Means |
|---|---|
| Bioenergetics | Studies **energy in the body**—how it's stored, moved, and used for healing. |
| Biogenetics | Studies **genes and DNA**—how traits are passed down from parents to kids. |

Think of it this way:

- **Bioenergetics = the energy running the system**
- **Biogenetics = the blueprint of the system**

Bioenergetics cares more about **how your energy flows**, while biogenetics cares more about **what your genes say**.

## How Did Tesla Use Bioenergetics?

Nikola Tesla never explicitly used the word "bioenergetics"—a term that would emerge decades later to describe the study of energy in living systems—but many of his ideas anticipated it in profound ways. Tesla's work with energy, frequency, and vibration was not just about powering machines. He believed that these forces also governed the *human body* and *mind*.

## 1. Tesla's Belief in the Body as an Electrical System

Tesla saw the human body as a conductor and generator of energy. He often compared it to an electrical circuit, capable of being tuned, disrupted, or recharged through energy. His belief that humans were energetic beings aligned with what we now understand as the **biofield**— the electromagnetic field that surrounds and interpenetrates the human body.

"If you could eliminate certain outside frequencies that interfered with our bodies, we would have greater resistance toward disease." – Nikola Tesla

That quote alone places him as a precursor to modern energy medicine.

## 2. Planetary Frequencies and Human Resonance

Tesla believed the Earth had a natural frequency (now known as the **Schumann resonance**, around 7.83 Hz) and that humans could harmonize with it. He designed experiments to try and tune into this frequency, imagining a future where people could restore balance in their body and mind simply by attuning to natural harmonics.

That idea lives on in today's **bioresonance therapies**, **grounding practices**, and even in technologies that aim to synchronize human energy fields with natural Earth frequencies.

### 3. Scalar Energy and Non-Local Healing

Tesla's theories of **scalar waves**—a type of energy that travels faster than light and does not diminish over distance—foreshadow today's concepts in **remote energy healing**. While science hasn't fully accepted scalar waves in mainstream physics, many energy medicine systems (like Reiki, Pranic Healing, and the work of Dr. Konstantin Korotkov in biofield imaging) are built on similar non-local principles.

Modern bioenergetic practices such as **distant healing**, **emotional field therapy**, or even **heart-brain coherence training** reflect Tesla's belief that energy could be transmitted wirelessly, instantly, and intentionally.

### 4. Tuning the Body Like a Resonant System

Tesla frequently described the universe as a giant system of frequencies and oscillations. He believed that if you could "tune" a system to the right frequency, healing or destruction could occur. That thinking now underpins:

- **Sound therapy**
- **Vibrational medicine**
- **Chakra tuning**
- **Tuning fork therapy**
- **Pulsed electromagnetic field (PEMF) therapy**

Tesla's coil wasn't just a device for electricity. It was a metaphor for the body as an instrument—one that, when properly tuned, could enter into energetic coherence and healing.

## 5. From Machines to Inner Technology

Although Tesla built machines, he also spoke of *invisible* forces—those tied to thought, intention, emotion, and spiritual connection. These align with the **inner technologies** used today in practices like:

- Breathwork
- Meditation
- Visualization
- Intention setting
- Energy mapping

Tesla believed the future of medicine would not be chemical but **vibrational**—a statement echoed today in integrative health circles and bioenergetic practices worldwide.

Tesla's contributions to what we now understand as **bioenergetics** were visionary, and many of today's frequency-based healing practices can trace their philosophical roots back to his experiments, ideas, and quotes.

# Chapter 2: Frequency, Coherence & the Language of the Body

## Understanding How Your Body Talks Through Energy

*H*ave you ever noticed how your mood can change just by listening to music? Or how being around someone who's super calm makes you feel relaxed too? That's frequency and coherence in action—even if you didn't realize it!

**What is Frequency?**

Think of frequency like a rhythm or a wave. Everything in life moves in waves—even your thoughts, your heartbeat, and your feelings. Your body and brain are full of tiny electrical signals, kind of like Wi-Fi. These signals make up your personal energy "frequency."

- **Happy thoughts?** Your frequency is smooth and high.
- **Stressed or angry?** Your frequency gets jagged or low. So frequency is kind of like your body's first language. Before you speak, your body *broadcasts* how you're feeling through energy.

## What is Coherence?

Coherence is when all the parts of your body's energy are working together—like a team moving in the same direction.

Imagine a marching band. If everyone is walking to the same beat, it looks and sounds amazing. But if everyone's out of sync, it's a total mess.

That's what coherence is like for your body. When your heart, brain, and breath are "marching" together, your energy field becomes strong and clear. You feel calm, focused, and confident.

## Why This Matters

Your body is always "talking" in energy, whether you know it or not. That's why:

- Animals sense when you're scared.
- People pick up on your vibe without a word.
- You feel tired around certain people, and energized around others.

This silent language is what Tesla called *vibration and frequency*. It's the secret behind how healing really works—by helping your body remember its natural rhythm.

## In Simple Terms:

- **Frequency** is how your energy *sounds*.
- **Coherence** is how your energy *feels* when everything works in harmony.
- When you're in sync, your body *heals* better, *thinks* clearer, and *feels* more alive.

# How to Tune Your Energy

*(Even When You're Having a Bad Day)*

You don't have to be perfect to stay in a good energy flow. Life gets messy! But the cool part is—just like tuning a guitar—you can tune your energy anytime.

Here are a few simple ways to bring your body back into harmony:

### 1. Breathe Like You Mean It

Your breath is like a remote control for your nervous system. Try this:

- Breathe in for 4 counts.
- Hold for 4 counts.
- Breathe out for 4 counts.
- Do it 4 times.
  This is called a "coherence breath," and it helps your brain and heart sync up like best friends.

### 2. Think a Loving Thought

One kind thought can change your entire frequency. Try thinking of someone you love—or a pet, or a happy memory—and notice how your body relaxes. That's real-time frequency shift!

### 3. Get in Nature

The Earth has a rhythm called the Schumann Resonance. When you walk barefoot on the grass, hug a tree, or sit near a river, your body naturally matches that peaceful frequency.

### 4. Use Sound or Music

Play music that lifts you up—your cells are literally listening! Humming, chanting, or listening to soft tones helps bring your body into coherence.

### 5. Smile (Even if You Don't Feel Like It)

Smiling sends signals to your brain that say, "Hey, we're okay." It releases feel-good chemicals and lifts your frequency.

### A Quick Energy Check-In

Next time you're feeling off, ask yourself:

- Is my energy **low** or **high**?
- Is it **scattered** or **focused**?
- Do I feel **in sync**, or like everything's out of tune?

Then try one of the tuning tools above—and give your body a new rhythm to follow.

# Chapter 3: Bioenergetic Systems — Chakras, Meridians & the Tesla Lens

## How Ancient Wisdom And Modern Science Connect To Your Energy Flow

*L*et's back up a bit… Imagine Your Body Like a Super Cool Circuit Board

Have you ever looked at the inside of a computer or game console? It's full of pathways, wires, and energy moving around in all directions to keep everything running smoothly.

Your body has something very similar—only it's made of energy, not wires.

**"The Body as a Resonant Circuit"** Nikola Tesla believed that the human body could operate like a finely tuned electrical circuit—receiving, transmitting, and resonating with frequencies in nature. Just like a Tesla coil amplifies energy, he believed our bodies could amplify healing when tuned properly.

**Meet the Chakras and Meridians** *(way before Tesla)*

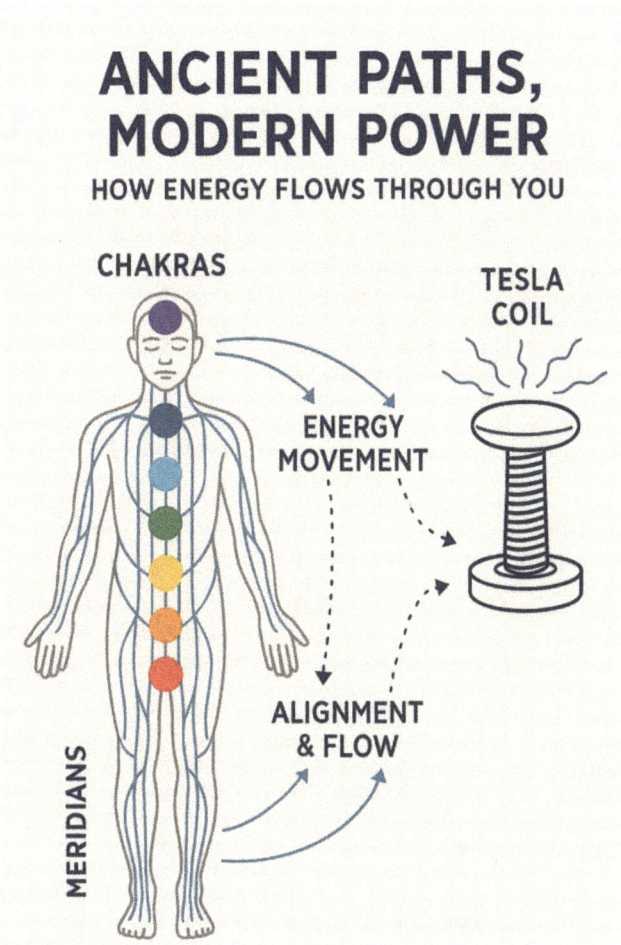

ANCIENT PATHS, MODERN POWER

HOW ENERGY FLOWS THROUGH YOU

CHAKRAS

TESLA COIL

ENERGY MOVEMENT

ALIGNMENT & FLOW

MERIDIANS

**Chakras** are like spinning energy wheels located in different parts of your body.

You've got seven main ones, from the base of your spine to the top of your head. Each chakra helps control parts of your life—like your voice, emotions, confidence, or even how creative you feel.

**Meridians** are energy highways, kind of like roads that connect your body's neighborhoods. These come from

Traditional Chinese Medicine, and they carry life energy (called *Qi* or *Chi*) to all your organs and systems.

Just like Wi-Fi signals or power lines, these systems help your "inner tech" stay connected and balanced.

## Tesla's Way of Thinking

Nikola Tesla—yes, the guy who inspired electric cars— believed everything in the universe works through **energy, frequency, and vibration.** He said, if you want to understand the world, don't just look at what you can touch. Look at the invisible forces too.

Tesla wasn't talking about chakras or meridians specifically, but his *ideas about energy* match really well. He believed the human body worked like a **bioelectric system**, which means energy moves through you the same way electricity flows through a machine.

So, when we combine **chakras, meridians**, and **Tesla's lens**, we get a whole new way to see the human body— not just as bones and muscles, but as an energy-powered masterpiece.

## Why This Matters

When your chakras or meridians are **blocked or out of sync**, it's like a video buffering or a phone on 1% battery. Your emotions, focus, and even your health can feel off.

But when your energy is **flowing right**, you feel like the best version of yourself—clear, creative, calm, and powerful.

## Real Talk: You Are Electric

Every emotion, every thought, every movement—you guessed it—has a frequency.
Learning how to tune into these systems gives you the power to:

- Understand how your body is feeling (before you even get sick)
- Recharge your energy like a Tesla coil
- Use tools like breathwork, sound, or even crystals to stay in balance
- Become your own energy healer

## Prompt: "How to Tune Your Circuit"

## Try This: Chakra-Meridian Wake-Up

1. Sit quietly and take a few deep breaths.
2. Rub your hands together to activate energy.
3. Place your hands over your heart (heart chakra and heart meridian).
4. Visualize golden light radiating outward, syncing like a pulse.
5. Breathe slowly and say, "I am aligned. I am in flow."
6. Notice how you feel—any tingles, warmth, or calm? That's your energy field tuning in.

Next up, we'll dive deeper into how to actually *read* your energy field—like scanning your inner Wi-Fi for strength bars. But first, just remember:

You're not just skin and bones.
You're *energy in motion*.

# Chapter 4: Natural Intelligence vs. Artificial Intelligence

## The Conscious Field vs. the Programmed Machine

$7$n an era captivated by the rapid rise of Artificial Intelligence (AI), it is easy to overlook the profound mystery and power of our own *Natural Intelligence* (NI). Tesla's vision—rooted in frequency, vibration, and resonance—did not depend on silicon chips or machine learning algorithms. It flowed from the understanding that the human being is both receiver and transmitter of subtle energy: a living bioenergetic system with the capacity to *heal, evolve, and create.*

This book introduces **Natural Intelligence** as the self-organizing, sentient energetic field that animates life. It's the intelligence that governs cellular communication, restores coherence during healing, and guides intuitive insight. It is embodied in your nervous system, expressed through your biofield, and accessible through energetic awareness.

By contrast, **Artificial Intelligence** is a product of human ingenuity—designed to replicate logical tasks, process massive datasets, and increasingly mimic decision-making. But it remains external. It cannot *feel* coherence, nor can it *initiate* frequency-based healing. AI can recognize your symptoms, but it cannot touch your soul.

## Why This Matters in Bioenergetics

As practitioners of energy medicine, it is vital to understand the limits and possibilities of both realms:

| Natural Intelligence (NI) | Artificial Intelligence (AI) |
|---|---|
| Emerges from the living field | Emerges from programming |
| Supports intuition, coherence, and energetic healing | Supports logic, prediction, and pattern recognition |
| Evolves with consciousness | Evolves with data inputs |
| Informed by soul, spirit, and energetic lineage | Informed by machine learning models |
| Accessible through meditation, breath, touch, vibration | Accessible through interfaces and code |
| Works in harmony with Tesla's frequency-based principles | May simulate but not generate frequency fields |

NI is the future of human evolution—not something to replace, but something to reclaim. As Tesla once said, "If you want to find the secrets of the universe, think in terms of energy, frequency, and vibration."

This book offers a blueprint for restoring coherence in the human system—not by outsourcing our power to AI, but by awakening the Natural Intelligence already within us.

# Natural Intelligence: A Lifespan Perspective

While Artificial Intelligence is engineered, trained, and coded through logic and data, **Natural Intelligence (NI)** is the inherent, self-organizing energy system present in all living beings. It cannot be manufactured, yet it organizes breath, emotion, healing, coherence, and consciousness.

Natural Intelligence isn't learned—it's remembered. It's already inside us, quietly operating beneath our thoughts. The more we strip away distractions, conditioning, and misalignment, the more we return to this pure intelligence.

Let's look at how NI expresses itself naturally through different life stages:

### The Newborn: Instinctual Energy & Unfiltered Sensitivity

- **Natural Intelligence at its rawest form.**
- A newborn cries when hungry, sleeps when tired, turns away from overstimulation, and reaches toward warmth and comfort.
- They don't question their needs or suppress their emotions.
- They pick up on unseen frequencies—emotional states, energetic fields, and resonance—often more accurately than adults.

- Their energy body is open, unblocked, and highly intuitive.

*This is the body in its purest energetic coherence. No doubt. No delay. No disconnection.*

### The Child: Curiosity, Movement & Energy Expression

- Children move constantly—not just to burn energy, but to process it.
- They ask questions not to challenge, but to **understand meaning**. Natural Intelligence drives learning through curiosity, not data retention.
- They act out emotions through the body— throwing, running, dancing, yelling, crying— expressing the energy that adults have learned to suppress.
- Touch, play, sound, and imagination are all active NI tools at this age.

*They don't think about regulating energy—they do it naturally.*

### The Teenager: Conflict Between Conditioning and Truth

- Here, **NI begins to compete with social programming**. Teens may "know" what's true in their body (gut instincts, emotional urges), but societal expectations often force them to suppress or second-guess it.
- They start feeling "off" when forced to conform to systems that ignore emotional and energetic realities.
- Intuition is strong—but often overridden by fear of rejection or failure.
- Physical symptoms (migraines, stomach aches, anxiety) are often NI trying to speak.

*This is where many begin to disconnect from Natural Intelligence to "fit in."*

### The Adult: Reclaiming or Ignoring Inner Wisdom

- Adults often live in a state of dissonance between what their body knows and what their mind has been trained to believe.
- **Reconnection** to Natural Intelligence may come through healing, trauma recovery, meditation, breathwork, energy work, or breakdowns that force a "reset."
- Once reconnected, adults may realize they've been living out of coherence—ignoring their energy field's messages in favor of external validation.

*Healing is not about "learning more"—it's about* **remembering and trusting what was always inside.**

Natural Intelligence is not mystical—it is biological, energetic, and **universal**. Whether through instinct, emotion, or subtle perception, our human energy system is a self-organizing blueprint designed to restore balance, connection, and vitality.

As Tesla once said, "If you want to find the secrets of the universe, think in terms of energy, frequency, and vibration." The body already knows this. We just need to listen.

# Chapter 5: The Body as a Bioelectric Field

*T*he **human biofield** is an invisible but powerful energy field that surrounds and interpenetrates your physical body. Imagine your body is like a phone that runs on **energy** — not just food, but **electrical energy** too.

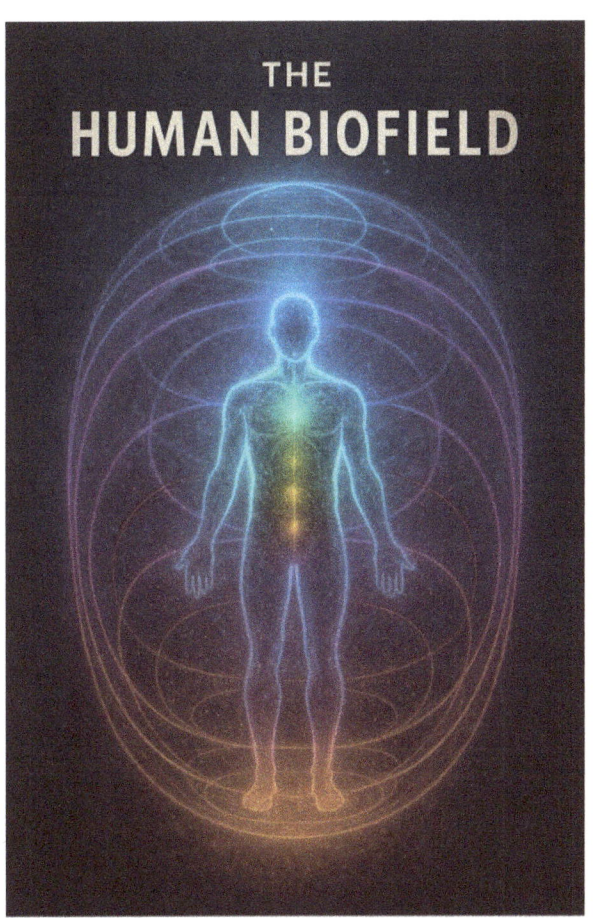

Every time you **move your muscles, think a thought**, or even **feel an emotion**, your body sends little electrical signals through your nerves and brain. These tiny signals are **bioelectricity** — a natural kind of energy your body makes and uses to stay alive and healthy.

Now here's the cool part:
All those tiny signals add up and create a kind of **energy field** around your body. You can't see it, but it's always there — kind of like Wi-Fi or the glow from your phone screen.

This invisible energy around you is called your **biofield** or **bioelectric field**. It helps:

- Keep your body in balance
- Guide healing
- Let cells "talk" to each other

Scientists are starting to understand that your **energy field affects your health** — and if that field gets out of balance, you might feel tired, stressed, or even get sick.

Just like a phone needs a good **signal** and full **battery**, your body needs a strong, balanced energy field to feel your best.

That's why learning how to care for your energy (using things like breathwork, sound, light, and intention) is just as important as eating healthy or exercising.

Let's think about your phone a bit more...

- If your battery dies, your phone shuts off.
- If you have no signal, you can't send messages, watch videos, or get on TikTok.

It might still look fine on the outside—but without power and connection, it's useless.

Well, your **body works the same way**.

You're not just skin, bones, and muscles. You're also full of **energy**—a natural current that flows through your body like electricity through wires.

This energy field (sometimes called your **biofield**) is what helps your body and mind stay balanced, focused, and healthy. It powers how you feel, think, and even how your body heals itself.

So…

- When your energy is *strong and balanced*, you feel good. You think clearly. You sleep better. You bounce back faster from stress.
- When your energy is *weak, scattered, or blocked*, you might feel tired, sad, anxious, moody, or even sick.

This book is all about **how to charge your "inner battery"** and tune your body's signal—just like keeping your phone fully juiced and connected.

Except this time, *you* are the smart device.

Let's learn how to power up your body's energy system the way Tesla might have imagined it—through frequency, harmony, and the invisible forces that connect us all.

For a deeper insight into how energy really works in the body, you're invited to watch:

Proof of Energy Experiment #1
With Dr. Constance Santego
https://youtu.be/jnZAOGYWy2M

And #2

https://youtu.be/0mEXbz11LME

In the video you'll see a live experiment that brings to life many of the concepts in this chapter—watch how subtle signals show up in the field, how coherence changes the system, and how you might begin to sense your own bioelectric potential.

Feel free to pause, rewind, and reflect as you go through it. Use it as a visual anchor to what you're reading—and a chance to feel your own field in action.

# How Science Measures the Biofield

Until recently, energy medicine was brushed off as "woo." But thanks to technological breakthroughs, science is finally catching up with what ancient traditions always knew.

Here are **three modern tools** now used to measure and explore the biofield:

### 1. Heart Rate Variability (HRV) – HeartMath Institute

Your heart isn't just a pump—it's a powerful electrical organ that communicates with your brain and body through electromagnetic waves. **HRV** measures the variation in time between heartbeats. A high HRV indicates emotional resilience and energetic balance. Low HRV? Stress, burnout, or illness.

*HeartMath's research shows that a calm, coherent heart rhythm positively impacts your entire biofield.*

### 2. Electroencephalogram (EEG) – Brainwave Scanning

EEGs measure the electrical activity of your brain. When your biofield is balanced, your brain tends to produce calm, focused waves like alpha or theta. Stress and trauma show up as chaotic beta waves. Advanced EEG mapping can now show how breath, meditation, sound therapy, and even intention shift the brain—and the field.

### 3. Gas Discharge Visualization (GDV) – Biophoton Imaging

Also known as the **Kirlian Effect**, GDV scans measure the photon emissions (light particles) released from your skin—especially from your fingers. These glowing images reveal the energy field's shape, strength, and disruptions. They can reflect areas of tension, emotional imbalance, and physical disease—before symptoms even show up in the body.

# Why Frequency Healing Is the Medicine of the Future

As the world races toward more advanced technologies, humanity is beginning to rediscover something ancient— something encoded in the body itself. While Artificial Intelligence and robotic surgeries make headlines, a quiet revolution is taking place in the world of healing— through frequency.

The future of medicine won't be dominated solely by machines, but by harmonizing the **subtle energies of the human biofield**.

In traditional medicine, we often wait until something breaks before fixing it. Frequency healing flips this model. It's not just reactive; it's **proactive, preventative, and profoundly personalized**. It taps into **resonance**—the same principle that allows a tuning fork to vibrate another one nearby without touching it. In healing, the right frequency can gently shift tissues, emotions, and even thoughts into alignment—no pills, no side effects, no invasive procedures.

What Makes This the Future?

- **Instant Biofeedback:** Technologies like PEMF, sound baths, Rife machines, and Tesla coils now give us the power to measure, emit, and adjust frequency fields. Imagine a world where your stress isn't managed by pharmaceuticals but by a **vibrational tune-up.**

- **Quantum Coherence:** Scientific studies now support the idea that cells communicate through more than just chemicals—they exchange **photons and frequencies.** Healing through frequency aligns the body at the speed of light, not just the speed of blood flow.

- **Accessibility & Affordability:** Unlike high-tech hospital procedures, frequency-based therapies can be practiced at home or in simple holistic clinics. These methods empower both practitioner and patient to become co-creators in the healing journey.

- **Consciousness Integration:** Perhaps most importantly, frequency medicine integrates **mind, body, and spirit.** It doesn't treat you like a broken machine—it reminds you that you are already whole, and helps you **resonate back to that truth.**

# Resonance vs. Resistance

*Energy flows where resonance goes.*

Imagine you're trying to ride a skateboard on a smooth sidewalk — it's easy, fun, and you glide effortlessly. That's **resonance**: when energy is aligned, smooth, and in flow.

Now imagine trying to ride that same skateboard on gravel or uphill. Every push is harder, slower, and frustrating. That's **resistance**: when energy is blocked, misaligned, or out of tune.

*What Is Resonance?*

Resonance is when two things naturally "vibe" together. Think of a singer breaking a glass with their voice — that's not magic, it's **resonance**. The voice hits the exact frequency the glass naturally vibrates at, and boom! It amplifies until the glass can't take it.

Your body does the same with people, sounds, and environments. When you hear your favorite song and feel energized? That's resonance. When someone walks in a room and you instantly feel calm or safe? Also resonance.

In healing, **resonance means alignment** — the right frequency hitting the right system to create balance.

*What Is Resistance?*

Resistance is when energy tries to move, but something pushes back. This can happen in your body, mind, or even your emotions.

Ever feel super tired after being around certain people? Or get a headache in noisy places? That's your energy

field hitting **resistance**. Something isn't harmonizing —
it's clashing, like two instruments playing different keys at
once.

In your body, resistance can show up as:

- Chronic pain
- Anxiety
- Mood swings
- Feeling stuck or tired for no reason

Resistance **blocks flow**. And without flow, the body can't
heal properly.

### Story: The Radio Inside You

Imagine you're a radio.

Not just any radio—one that plays the soundtrack of *you*.
Your hopes, your thoughts, your feelings. And just like a
real radio, your body needs to be *tuned* to the right station
to sound good.

Let's say your happy station is 101.5 FM. That's when
you're laughing with your friends, your body feels light,
your brain is clear, and things seem to flow. That's
*resonance*—you're in tune with yourself and the world
around you.

But have you ever turned the dial just a little and gotten
stuck between stations? Static. Muffled voices.
Frustration. That's *resistance*. The signal's there, but you're
not lined up with it. You can't hear the music because
you're not on the right frequency.

This happens in life, too.

- When you hang around people who make you feel drained or judged, that's resistance.
- When you ignore how tired or sad you are, and keep pushing through, that's resistance.
- When you say "yes" when you want to say "no," you're turning the dial off your own station.

But...

- When you listen to your gut and it feels right? That's resonance.
- When you walk into a room and feel like you belong, without trying? Resonance.
- When you're creative, rested, curious, and everything feels *easy*—you're tuned in.

Just like a crystal radio doesn't need batteries, only *alignment*, your body runs best when it's in harmony—resonating—not pushing against the signal.

**Tesla** believed the entire universe was made of energy, frequency, and vibration.

And you?

You're a walking, breathing frequency transmitter. Every thought, emotion, and action either helps your signal shine clearly—or scrambles it with static.

So next time you feel off, don't fight it. Pause. Breathe. Re-tune.

The music's still there. You just need to find your station again.

Healing is about tuning your body to **resonance** — like a perfectly tuned guitar string. When you're in resonance, your energy moves easily, your body feels light, your thoughts are clearer, and your emotions more balanced.

You don't need to force healing. You just need to remove resistance and allow the natural energy to **flow where resonance goes**.

# Resonance vs. Resistance: Real-Life Stories of Energy Flow

### 1. Emotional Resonance

**Story:**
Imagine you're feeling down—maybe a friend said something hurtful, and you're carrying that weight all day. Then your dog runs up to you with pure love, tail wagging like you're the best person in the world. Something shifts. That joy, even for a moment, lifts your energy.

**Explanation:**
Your dog's joyful energy *resonated* with a deeper part of you that remembered love and connection. That's emotional resonance. When you feel "seen" or "held" emotionally, your frequency rises.
But if you ignore the emotion, bottle it up, or surround yourself with people who criticize or judge, that's *resistance*—your energy contracts, and you feel drained or off.

**Key Takeaway:** Energy flows where it feels safe and seen. That's why a smile from someone who gets you can feel like medicine.

### 2. Physical Resonance

**Story:**
Ever notice how your body naturally starts moving to music you love? You tap your foot. Nod your head. Or get full-body goosebumps from a powerful song. That's your cells *resonating* with the frequency of the sound.

Now think of when you walk into a room that's stuffy, filled with fluorescent lights, maybe too cold or too noisy.

Your shoulders tense. Your breath shortens. Your energy *resists* the space.

**Explanation:**
Your physical body is always "reading" the frequencies around it. When something matches your system (resonance), your body feels at ease. When something clashes (resistance), you feel tight, tired, or even sick.

**Key Takeaway:** Your body is a tuning fork. Tune in to what makes it hum—not what makes it shrink.

## 3. Environmental Resonance

**Story:**
You go hiking. The trees sway gently. The air smells clean. You can hear birdsong and feel the earth beneath your feet. You take a deep breath—and something inside you calms. You're in *resonance* with nature.

Now picture yourself stuck in traffic. Horns blaring. People yelling. Asphalt heat radiating off the pavement. Your jaw clenches. You're irritated before you even arrive. That's *resistance*.

**Explanation:**
Nature has a naturally coherent frequency. When we're in it, our own energy field tends to sync up and regulate. But environments that are chaotic, polluted, or energetically "off" create friction in our system.

**Key Takeaway:** Where you place your body determines how your energy flows. Choose coherence over chaos when you can.

## Resonance Is the Language of Healing

When something resonates with you—be it a person, place, sound, scent, or even an idea—you feel open, connected, *whole*. That's what Tesla meant when he said to "understand the universe in terms of frequency and vibration."

Healing happens through *resonance*, not resistance.

Your job is to become the kind of person, practitioner, or presence that *radiates resonance*.

# Bioenergetics Healing Practices

## Energy-Based Therapies

These focus on the flow, balance, and coherence of the body's energy field (biofield).

### *What is an Energy-Based Therapy?*

An **energy-based therapy** is a healing method that works with the body's **natural energy field** (also called the *biofield*). These therapies aim to **balance, clear, and restore the flow of energy** to support physical, emotional, mental, and spiritual well-being. Practitioners often use their hands, breath, or intention to guide this energy—either by touching the body lightly or working just above it.

### Subcategories & Examples:

- **Reiki** – Channeling universal energy through hands to restore balance.
- **Healing Touch** – A medically accepted method of energy balancing through light touch.
- **Therapeutic Touch** – Developed by nurses to support healing by manipulating the energy field.
- **Quantum-Touch** – Uses breath and body awareness to raise vibration and affect healing.
- **Pranic Healing** – Cleansing and energizing the energy body using prana (life force).
- **Qi Gong Healing** – Ancient Chinese practice of moving qi through the body using breath, motion, and intention.
- **Polarity Therapy** – Balances positive and negative energy currents in the body using gentle manipulation.

## Historical Origin:

- **Reiki**: Originated in early 20th century Japan by Mikao Usui after a meditative experience on Mt. Kurama.
- **Healing Touch & Therapeutic Touch**: Developed in the 1970s–1980s in the U.S. by nurses like Dolores Krieger and Janet Mentgen, integrating ancient concepts into clinical practice.
- **Pranic Healing & Qi Gong**: Rooted in **ancient Chinese medicine** and **Hindu yogic traditions**, dating back over 2,000 years.
- **Polarity Therapy**: Created in the 1940s by Dr. Randolph Stone, blending Eastern and Western energetic principles.

## Tesla Alignment:

Energy-based therapies like **Reiki, Healing Touch, and Qi Gong** align closely with Tesla's views on the human body as a finely tuned energetic system. Tesla believed the body operated like an oscillating circuit, capable of being brought into balance through external frequencies. His work with scalar energy—non-Hertzian, subtle waves—supports the idea of transmitting healing energy without direct physical contact, a hallmark of modalities like Therapeutic Touch and Quantum-Touch. The high-vibrational coherence sought in these practices echoes Tesla's principle of restoring health through resonance and energetic harmony, using frequencies to re-establish the natural biofield rhythm of the body.

Safety & Ethics Notes:

- ✅ *Safe for most people*, including children, elderly, and animals.
- ❌ *Should not replace medical treatment* for serious conditions—use as complementary care.
- 🔒 Always **get consent** before placing hands on or near someone's body.
- ⚖️ Practitioners must stay grounded and emotionally neutral; projecting personal issues may interfere with energy flow.
- ⚠️ Some people may experience emotional release; support integration.

## Frequency and Vibration Therapies

These utilize specific frequencies or vibrations to align the energy field.

### *What is a Frequency or Vibration Therapy?*

A **frequency therapy** uses **specific sounds, tones, or electromagnetic vibrations** to bring the body into harmony. Every organ and system in the body has a natural frequency. When this frequency is disrupted, illness or imbalance can occur. These therapies aim to **restore that natural rhythm** using tools like sound bowls, tuning forks, or frequency-generating machines.

### Subcategories & Examples:

- **Tesla Frequency Therapy** – Uses scalar or vibrational waves inspired by Tesla's theories.
- **Rife Frequency Healing** – Applies electromagnetic frequencies to target pathogens or balance organs.
- **Bioresonance Therapy** – Detects and sends frequencies to restore harmony.
- **Tuning Fork Therapy** – Applies precise sound frequencies to specific points or meridians.
- **Vibrational Sound Therapy** – Includes gongs, crystal bowls, and chimes to align chakras and aura.
- **Solfeggio Frequencies** – Sacred frequencies believed to harmonize energy and DNA.

## Historical Origin:

- **Rife & Bioresonance**: Developed in the early to mid-20th century by Royal Rife (U.S.) and Franz Morell (Germany).
- **Tuning Forks & Sound Healing**: Have roots in ancient Egypt, Greece, and India, where sound was used in temples and rituals.
- **Solfeggio Frequencies**: Derived from Gregorian chants and early Christian hymns dating to medieval Europe.
- **Tesla Frequency Therapy**: Inspired by Tesla's 1890s work with electromagnetic fields and harmonic resonance.

## Tesla Alignment:

Tesla often said, *"If you want to understand the universe, think in terms of energy, frequency, and vibration."* He viewed vibration as the **carrier of resonance**, and much like how his devices harnessed harmonic frequencies, these therapies use sound to recalibrate the body's energetic field. Tesla's experiments with **scalar waves**, **resonant circuits**, and **high-voltage, low-current energy** form the foundation of many frequency-based devices. He believed the body could be tuned like an oscillating circuit—resonating at ideal frequencies for health. Scalar energy (non-Hertzian waves) is directly attributed to Tesla and underlies many modern energy healing devices.

**Safety & Ethics Notes:**

- ✅ Non-invasive, but effects can be powerful—start slow and observe responses.
- ❌ Avoid in **pregnancy, epilepsy, pacemakers**, or with implanted electrical devices unless cleared.
- ⚠️ Use frequency ranges **appropriate for age, condition, and need** (overstimulation can cause headaches or agitation).
- 🧠 Respect **mental-emotional states**—certain tones can stir subconscious or trauma-related energy.
- 👂 Never use tuning forks or loud sound near the ears without proper technique.

## Light, Color, and Magnetism Therapies
(Photobiomodulation)

Using photonic or electromagnetic tools to affect energy.

### What is a Light, Color, or Magnetism Therapy?

This group uses **light waves, color frequencies, and magnetic fields** to support healing at the cellular or energetic level. These therapies are often **non-invasive** and use tools like lasers, red lights, or magnets to stimulate the body's natural repair systems and restore energetic flow.

### Subcategories & Examples:

- **Color Therapy (Chromotherapy)** – Using specific colors to treat different ailments and chakras.
- **Laser Acupuncture** – Applying low-level light to acupuncture points.
- **Red Light Therapy (LLLT)** – Penetrates tissues to promote healing and cellular repair.
- **Magnet Therapy** – Uses magnetic fields to relieve pain or rebalance biofield polarity.
- **Pulsed Electromagnetic Field (PEMF) Therapy** – Emits pulsed magnetic waves to stimulate cellular energy.

## Historical Origin:

- **Color Therapy**: Practiced in **Ancient Egypt, India (Ayurveda)**, and **Greece** using colored light and crystals.
- **Magnet Therapy**: Found in early **Chinese and Indian medical texts**, over 2,000 years ago.
- **Red Light & Laser Therapy**: Developed from 1960s space research (NASA), later integrated into therapeutic medicine.

## Tesla Alignment:

Tesla worked extensively with **light frequencies** and color, creating artificial sunlight through his high-voltage experiments. He was fascinated by how **color and light interacted with biological systems**, and today's color therapy echoes his belief that each frequency of light holds specific healing properties.

## Safety & Ethics Notes:

- ✖ Avoid direct light therapy **on eyes** or over **cancerous tumors**, **thyroid**, or **pregnant abdomen**.
- ⚡ PEMF and magnet therapy should **not be used on people with pacemakers**, defibrillators, or certain metal implants.
- 💡 Observe **exposure times and dosage**—more is not always better.
- ✅ Color therapy is generally safe, but emotional sensitivity to color shifts can occur—watch for mood changes.

## Plant & Nature-Based Bioenergetics

Harnessing vibrational qualities of plants and natural elements.

### What is a Plant & Nature-Based Bioenergetic Therapy?

These methods work with the **vibrational qualities of plants and nature**. It's not about the chemical ingredients of herbs or oils—but rather their **energetic imprint**. These subtle frequencies are believed to support emotional healing, raise your vibration, and bring balance to your energy field.

### Subcategories & Examples:

- **Flower Essences** (e.g., Bach Remedies) – Carry the vibrational imprint of flowers to shift emotional states.
- **Essential Oils** – Used in aromatherapy for emotional and energetic alignment.
- **Floraopathy™** (your modality) – Applying plant frequency and intention for targeted energy work.

### Historical Origin:

- **Flower Essences**: Popularized in the 1930s by **Dr. Edward Bach** in England.
- **Essential Oils**: Used for over 5,000 years in **Egyptian, Persian, Indian (Ayurveda)**, and **Traditional Chinese Medicine**.
- **Floraopathy™**: A modern integrative modality blending Tesla principles with botanical frequencies.

### Tesla Alignment:

Nikola Tesla believed that everything in nature vibrates at its own frequency, and that these frequencies can influence the human biofield. He viewed nature as a powerful conduit of energy, and his studies into resonance, energy transmission, and scalar waves directly support the idea that plants emit subtle vibrational patterns. In plant-based bioenergetics, such as flower essences, essential oils, and Floraopathy™, this understanding is reflected in the use of plant frequencies to influence emotional and energetic well-being. Tesla's insights into non-Hertzian energy and the energetic resonance of matter offer a foundational explanation for how natural substances can imprint their frequency onto the body's field—facilitating healing without physical or biochemical interaction.

### Safety & Ethics Notes:

- ❌ **Essential oils are potent**—never ingest unless trained; dilute before topical use.
- 🌸 Be aware of **allergies**, especially with sensitive skin or respiratory conditions.
- ⚖️ Choose **ethical sourcing** for plant materials—sustainability matters.
- 🌸 Emotional reactions may surface with vibrational remedies—support the process, don't rush it.
- 🪔 Always **test for sensitivity** before full application, especially with children or pets.

# Mind-Body Energy Techniques

Psychological-emotional release methods that work through energy pathways.

### *What is a Mind-Body Energy Technique?*

These techniques combine **emotional healing and energy work**, based on the belief that emotions and thoughts create energetic imprints in the body. They use tapping, breathing, visualization, or muscle testing to **release emotional blocks** and rewire limiting beliefs— supporting deep transformation.

### Subcategories & Examples:

- **Emotional Freedom Technique (EFT / Tapping)** – Uses acupressure points while speaking affirmations.
- **Psych-K** – Belief-change protocol using muscle testing and energetic balancing.
- **ESR (Emotional Stress Release)** – Touching specific points to discharge emotional energy.
- **Somatic Experiencing** – Releases trauma stored in the nervous system and energy field.
- **Matrix Reimprinting** – Advanced EFT that works within the energetic memory field.

### Historical Origin:

- **EFT / Matrix Reimprinting**: Developed by Gary Craig in the 1990s, inspired by Thought Field Therapy by Dr. Roger Callahan.
- **Psych-K**: Created by Rob Williams in the late 1980s.
- **Somatic Experiencing**: Developed by Dr. Peter Levine based on his work in trauma recovery and nervous system regulation.

- **Emotional Stress Release (ESR)**: Evolved from kinesiology and mind-body integration models in the 1970s.

## Tesla Alignment:

Tesla's view of the universe as a frequency-based system aligns with mind-body energy methods that tap into the body's electromagnetic and bio-informational networks. His belief that thoughts are vibrational and that the brain is both a transmitter and receiver of frequencies resonates with modalities like EFT, Psych-K, and Matrix Reimprinting, which operate on the principle that changing internal energy patterns can shift physical and emotional health. These techniques often use light touch, intention, and energetic pathways—mirroring Tesla's ideas of resonance, entrainment, and frequency modulation as tools for transformation and healing.

## Safety & Ethics Notes:

- ✅ Safe and empowering for most people, but some trauma release methods should be guided by trained practitioners.
- ❌ Don't force memory recall or regression—respect readiness.
- 👥 Consent, confidentiality, and emotional safety are crucial—these methods often involve sensitive belief work.
- ⚠️ Be cautious with individuals in active psychiatric crises—refer out when necessary.
- 🧘 Integration support (rest, journaling, grounding) is encouraged after sessions.

# Biofeedback & Muscle Testing

These interpret energy responses to stimuli for healing direction.

## What is Biofeedback & Muscle Testing?

Biofeedback and muscle testing are tools that **interpret the body's energetic responses** to different stimuli. They help practitioners discover where the body is out of balance or under stress—**without needing lab tests or machines**. Muscle testing is like asking your body yes/no questions and watching how it responds.

## Subcategories & Examples:

- **Kinesiology (Touch for Health, Applied Kinesiology)** – Tests muscle strength as energetic indicator.
- **Heart Rate Variability Biofeedback** – Measures coherence between heart and brain.
- **Electrodermal Screening** – Detects electrical conductance of skin for energetic stress.

## Historical Origin:

- **Kinesiology**: Applied Kinesiology was founded in 1964 by Dr. George Goodheart, building on chiropractic models.
- **HRV Biofeedback**: Emerged in the 1990s with advances in neurocardiology and heart-brain coherence (HeartMath Institute).
- **Electrodermal Screening**: Originates from **Dr. Reinhold Voll's** work in Germany (1950s), connecting acupuncture points with electrical resistance.

**Tesla Alignment:**

Tesla's innovations in electrical resonance and sensitivity to vibrational feedback laid the groundwork for understanding how the body responds to subtle energetic changes. Just as Tesla's coils detected energetic fluctuations and transmitted invisible frequencies, biofeedback and muscle testing rely on the body's immediate energetic responses to stimuli—like a living antenna system. Techniques such as kinesiology, HRV biofeedback, and electrodermal screening operate on principles similar to Tesla's belief in a reactive, frequency-based biofield, detecting stress patterns and coherence shifts that inform healing decisions.

**Safety & Ethics Notes:**

- ⚖️ Must be performed by **trained individuals** to ensure accurate, non-biased results.
- ❌ Muscle testing can be inaccurate during dehydration, stress, or fatigue—verify with repeated testing or additional methods.
- 📈 Devices like HRV monitors should not be used to self-diagnose conditions—use for awareness and lifestyle shifts.
- 🤲 Always obtain **informed consent** before testing, especially with physical contact.
- 🧪 These are **indirect diagnostic tools**—never claim to diagnose or cure disease.

## Sacred & Esoteric Modalities

Ancient and spiritually rooted systems for working with energy.

### What is a Sacred or Esoteric Energy Modality?

These are energy practices rooted in **ancient spiritual systems** and mysticism. They work with invisible forces like *chakras*, *meridians*, or *spirit energy* and often involve rituals, symbols, crystals, or intuitive guidance. They blend energy work with **sacred traditions** and the unseen world.

### Subcategories & Examples:

- **Chakra Therapy** – Balancing the seven main energy centers of the body.
- **Meridian Therapy** – Based on Traditional Chinese Medicine's energy pathways.
- **Shamanic Energy Healing** – Includes soul retrieval, cord clearing, and spirit-based diagnosis.
- **Crystal Healing** – Uses the vibrational signatures of crystals for specific energetic effects.
- **Scalar Energy Healing** – Uses longitudinal waves to influence subtle fields.

### Historical Origin:

- **Chakras & Meridians**: **Ancient India (Vedas)** and **China (TCM)** respectively, over 2,000 years ago.
- **Shamanic Energy Healing**: Prehistoric roots— found in **Indigenous cultures worldwide** (e.g., Peru, Mongolia, Siberia).
- **Crystal Healing**: Used by **Ancient Egyptians, Mayans, Greeks, and Native American tribes**.

- **Scalar Healing**: Conceptualized more recently through reinterpretation of **Tesla's** scalar wave theories with esoteric frameworks.

## Tesla Alignment:

Nikola Tesla's work suggested that the universe is composed of subtle energies beyond the electromagnetic spectrum—energies he explored through scalar waves and non-Hertzian fields. These ideas closely mirror ancient esoteric traditions that describe prana, chi, or spiritual light as life-force energies that flow through and around the human body. Tesla's resonance and frequency theories align with chakra therapy (which tunes the energetic centers like oscillators), meridian pathways (comparable to his circuits and energy flow models), and even scalar energy healing (a direct use of Tesla's namesake waveforms). His belief in tuning the human body like a resonant system echoes the sacred geometries, vibrations, and crystal frequencies used in these modalities. Tesla's vision of a vibrational universe brings scientific credibility to what ancient systems have long practiced through intention, symbolism, and sacred ritual.

**Safety & Ethics Notes:**

- ⊙ Respect **spiritual and cultural origins**—don't appropriate without honoring lineages.

- ✅ Safe for most people, but some clients may be uncomfortable with mystical language—explain clearly and respectfully.

- 🌀 Energetic releases (crying, visions, body movements) can occur—create a safe, grounded container.

- ⚠️ Use discernment with **cord cutting or soul retrieval** techniques—only trained practitioners should facilitate.

- 🔒 Use **ethics in energetic boundaries**—never interfere with someone's field without permission.

## Modern Devices & Wearables

Technology-enhanced methods to influence or monitor the biofield.

### *What is a Modern Bioenergetics Device or Wearable?*

These are **technology-based tools** that help you **read, monitor, or correct your energy field**. Some scan your biofield and show energy imbalances on a screen. Others send frequencies or microcurrents back to the body to promote balance and healing. They're like **energy medicine gadgets** you can use at home or in clinics.

### Subcategories & Examples:

- **Bio-Well / GDV Cameras** – Measure aura and energy field changes.
- **Healy Device** – Delivers microcurrent and frequencies based on quantum sensors.
- **NES Health System** – Scans energetic distortions and delivers corrective infoceuticals.
- **PEMF Mats (e.g., BEMER)** – Used for circulation, vitality, and energetic grounding.

### Historical Origin:

- **Bio-Well**: Based on Gas Discharge Visualization developed by **Dr. Konstantin Korotkov** in Russia (1990s), building on Kirlian photography.
- **Healy / NES**: Developed in the 2000s–2010s using quantum information fields and microcurrent therapy, influenced by **quantum biology** and **bio-informational theories**.
- **PEMF Devices**: Originated from 20th-century research in **NASA, Eastern Europe, and Germany** for tissue regeneration and circulation.

## Tesla Alignment:

Tesla's visionary work laid the foundation for modern bioenergetic technologies by exploring how subtle energies could interact with living systems. His inventions involving oscillating electromagnetic fields, resonant frequency circuits, and non-Hertzian scalar waves are echoed in modern devices such as PEMF mats and Healy frequency tools. Tesla envisioned energy as the true medicine of the future—non-invasive, vibrational, and intelligently targeted. Devices like the Bio-Well, NES Health, and PEMF systems harness principles Tesla introduced, using frequency, coherence, and quantum information to scan or stimulate the body's energetic field. These technologies manifest Tesla's belief that energy, frequency, and vibration are the fundamental keys to health and healing.

## Safety & Ethics Notes:

- ⚠ Read **manufacturer guidelines and contraindications** carefully.
- ✖ Many are **not approved by regulatory agencies (FDA, Health Canada)**—cannot claim to treat or cure.
- 🔌 Do not use devices around **pacemakers, during pregnancy, or with seizures**, unless explicitly permitted.
- ⚗ Calibrate and clean devices regularly to ensure accuracy and hygiene.
- 💻 *Do not rely solely on machines*—always interpret results in context with client history and intuition.

# PART II — THE ENERGENEIC MAPPING METHOD

# Chapter 6: The Energeneic Mapping: Zones of the Energy Field

*I*magine your body is surrounded by invisible layers of energy that stretch out like a personal force field. This isn't science fiction – it's what researchers and practitioners in the fields of energy medicine and bioenergetics refer to as the **human energy field**, or more commonly, the **biofield**. Within this field, specific zones correspond to different aspects of your physical, emotional, mental, and spiritual well-being.

The **Energeneic Mapping** is a Tesla-inspired framework that maps the human energy field into organized zones. These zones are not random; they are deeply interconnected with known energetic systems like chakras, meridians, and auric layers – but also integrate frequency-based insights inspired by Nikola Tesla's work on vibration and field coherence.

## The Purpose of Energeneic Mapping

Energeneic Mapping is a technique used to identify, track, and rebalance areas within these energy zones. Just as a topographical map shows peaks and valleys, Energeneic Mapping reveals where your energy is flowing harmoniously – and where it may be blocked, depleted, or chaotic.

By applying frequency tools (like tuning forks, magnets, or essential oils), gentle touch, and intuitive perception, a practitioner can work with these zones to restore coherence. The result? Increased vitality, emotional balance, and greater access to intuition and creativity.

# The 7 Energeneic Zones

Each of these zones corresponds loosely with traditional chakra locations but expands their meaning to include field dynamics, resonance, and Tesla-style frequency interpretation:

1. **Root Zone (Survival Field)**
   o   Base of spine to knees; linked to stability, grounding, physical safety.
   o   Disruptions often reflect fear, insecurity, or disconnection from the body.
2. **Sacral Zone (Flow Field)**
   o   Hips to lower belly; governs pleasure, boundaries, creativity, and sensuality.
   o   Distortions show up as control issues, suppressed emotion, or guilt.
3. **Solar Plexus Zone (Power Field)**
   o   Midsection; center of personal power, motivation, and self-esteem.
   o   Resistance here can signal burnout, anger, or fear of success.
4. **Heart Zone (Coherence Field)**
   o   Center of the chest; the bridge between upper and lower energy fields.
   o   When coherent, this zone radiates love, forgiveness, and connection.
5. **Throat Zone (Expression Field)**
   o   Governs voice, self-expression, and clarity of purpose.

o   Imbalances may manifest as sore throats, tension, or withheld truth.

6. **Brow Zone (Perception Field)**
   o   Also known as the third eye; linked to intuition, insight, and imagination.
   o   Foggy thinking, headaches, or fear of seeing the truth can appear here.

7. **Crown Zone (Connection Field)**
   o   Top of the head; associated with purpose, inspiration, and divine connection.
   o   Disturbance may present as spiritual disconnection, cynicism, or despair.

## How Practitioners Use the Mapping

In Energeneic sessions, practitioners learn to "read" these zones through muscle testing, palpation, and subtle sensing. Much like reading a diagnostic scan, the practitioner assesses the field for:

- Congestion (stagnant energy)
- Deflation (energy loss)
- Fragmentation (split signals)
- Overcharge (hyperactivity or stress buildup)

Once identified, imbalances are addressed with tailored interventions such as:

- Breath and tone techniques
- Emotional Stress Release (ESR)
- Application of specific frequencies (sound, magnetics, light)
- Energetic affirmations and focused intention

The Energeneic Mapping provides a structured, intuitive map to navigate the complex interplay between body, mind, and energy – allowing Tesla-inspired healing to become a grounded, repeatable practice.

# Chapter 7: Muscle Testing as a Bioenergetic Feedback Tool

*M*uscle testing, also known as applied kinesiology, is a simple yet powerful way to tap into the body's bioenergetic intelligence. Think of it like a yes/no conversation with the energy system. When you apply gentle pressure to a muscle while asking a question or exposing the body to a substance, the body responds with either strength or weakness. This subtle shift can tell you a lot about internal stressors, imbalances, or energetic blockages.

## The Body Doesn't Lie

Unlike the conscious mind, which can rationalize or deny, the body gives real-time, unfiltered feedback. When an area of the body is energetically stressed, the electrical flow is disrupted, and the muscle tends to "unlock." This doesn't mean the muscle is weak—it means the energy system is responding with a signal that something isn't quite right.

## How It Works Energetically

Everything in the body is connected through energy channels, meridians, and electromagnetic fields. When you use muscle testing, you're essentially reading the body's field for stress, resonance, or misalignment. Just like tuning into a radio station, you're checking if the signal is clear or distorted. This makes muscle testing an ideal assessment method for the Energeneic Mapping process.

## Testing Techniques

There are several common methods:

- **Deltoid Arm Test**: The client extends their arm horizontally while the practitioner applies gentle downward pressure.
- **O-Ring Test**: The thumb and index finger are pressed together to form a circle, and the practitioner tries to pull them apart.
- **Self-Testing**: Advanced practitioners learn to use their own fingers, body sway, or tools like pendulums to test themselves.

## What You Can Test

- Emotional stress responses
- Food or environmental sensitivities
- Meridians and organ systems
- Effectiveness of a healing technique
- Energetic alignment of chakras
- Resonance with frequencies, oils, colors, or affirmations

## Ethics and Integrity

Because muscle testing accesses subconscious or energetic truths, it's important to approach it with clear intent, neutrality, and ethical responsibility. Practitioners must be aware of their own influence, biases, and emotional states, which can skew results.

## Integration with Tesla's Bioenergetic Blueprint

In this system, muscle testing becomes more than a diagnostic tool—it is a gateway into the Energeneic Mapping. Each test helps map which part of the energy field needs tuning, which frequencies resonate, and what techniques bring coherence. Combined with touch, sound, and intention, muscle testing helps decode the language of the body in real time.

*Muscle testing gives us a way to listen to the body's energy field. It's not about strength or weakness—it's about reading resonance. With training, it becomes one of the most precise tools in a Tesla-inspired healing practice.*

# Chapter 8: Emotional Frequency Storage & ESR

## How Emotion Lodges in Tissues

*I*magine your body is a recording device, constantly receiving and storing signals—not just physical sensations, but emotional ones too. When something intense happens—like a heartbreak, a shock, or even an overwhelming joy—your body doesn't always have the time or tools to process it right away. Instead, it stores that unprocessed emotional energy within the tissues, fascia, and energy field.

In bioenergetic terms, this is known as **emotional frequency storage**.

Each emotion vibrates at a unique frequency. Anger, for instance, carries a different energetic charge than grief or fear. If that emotional frequency isn't expressed, resolved, or metabolized through the energy system, it can become "stuck." These stuck frequencies often lodge themselves in specific zones of the body:

- **Grief** commonly nests in the lungs.
- **Anger** tends to hide in the liver.
- **Fear** settles into the kidneys.
- **Shame** embeds in the lower gut.
- **Heartbreak**—unsurprisingly—resides near the heart center.

Over time, these unresolved emotions can distort the flow of energy (your biofield), contribute to chronic tension or pain, and even alter posture or facial expressions. The body remembers what the mind forgets.

**ESR: Emotional Stress Release as a Clearing Protocol**

**ESR**, or **Emotional Stress Release**, is a powerful yet gentle method inspired by **Touch for Health** and now reimagined through the lens of **Tesla-inspired energy healing**. The goal of ESR is to **release stored emotional frequencies** from the tissues and nervous system using touch, intention, and entrainment.

 *The Core Principles of ESR:*

1. **Touch Activates Awareness**
   Lightly holding key neurovascular points on the forehead and/or specific energy meridian points helps to increase blood flow to the brain and brings emotional charge into conscious awareness.
2. **Breath Creates Coherence**
   Conscious breathing (slow and rhythmic) reestablishes heart-brain coherence, preparing the system to safely release stored emotions.
3. **Frequency Matches Unlock Stagnation**
   Using tuning forks, tonal humming, or subtle energy transmission while holding emotional trigger points helps match the stored frequency—bringing resonance to areas of resistance.
4. **Tesla's Contribution**
   By applying the principle that *"If you want to find the secrets of the universe, think in terms of energy, frequency, and vibration,"* we approach ESR as not just emotional clearing—but **vibrational recalibration**.

5. **Perception Transforms the Field**
   When a client recalls a memory or emotion during ESR and then views it from a new, empowered perspective (facilitated by the practitioner), it rewrites the energetic imprint.

## A Basic ESR Session Might Look Like:

- Begin with **muscle testing** to identify a priority emotional block.
- Ask the client to gently **hold frontal ESR points** with fingertips.
- Encourage deep, steady **breathing** while focusing on the issue.
- Use **tuning forks, Tesla coils, or subtle energetic touch** to vibrate the surrounding energy field.
- Guide the client through a short visualization or statement of release (e.g., "I no longer need to carry this.")
- End by **grounding the energy** with a sweep down the spine or auric field.

## ESR = Frequency Alchemy

Emotions aren't obstacles—they are messengers. ESR doesn't suppress emotion; it **transmutes** it. What was once stored as tension becomes transformed into energy, clarity, and flow.

In the Tesla-inspired model, ESR is **not just emotional healing**—it's the **alchemy of frequency**, where **stuck patterns are brought back into resonance with the true Self**.

# Chapter 9: Touch for Health — Realignment Through Movement & Touch

## Movement Is Medicine

*I*magine your energy field like a river system. If the flow becomes blocked—whether by injury, emotional stress, or stagnant posture—the "water" backs up, creating turbulence in the system. That turbulence often shows up as pain, tension, or chronic health issues.

The *Touch for Health* method combines physical movement, gentle touch, and muscle testing to realign this flow—almost like clearing the logjams in your body's energy streams.

Touching and moving the body in intentional ways doesn't just make your muscles feel better—it clears the static out of your energy field, helping restore natural harmony to your internal systems. Every stretch, posture shift, or tap has the potential to be a recalibration of energy.

### Resetting the Field Through the Body

Touch for Health, developed by John Thie and rooted in applied kinesiology, is based on the idea that the body *knows* how to heal when given the right nudge. That "nudge" can be a simple press on a neuro-lymphatic point, a spinal alignment move, or tracing a meridian line with your fingers.

When layered with *Tesla-style* frequency awareness, these movements take on even more power. You're not just activating physical pathways—you're tuning the entire electromagnetic field around you.

These gentle techniques offer an accessible way to:

- Rebalance organ energy via muscle-to-meridian correlations.
- Support emotional wellness by addressing the physical manifestations of stress.
- Improve posture and physical performance by restoring muscular integrity.

And the most beautiful part? The client's body leads the session. Your hands simply listen.

### Tesla Meets Touch

When Tesla spoke of energy, vibration, and frequency, he was referencing the invisible systems underlying everything. *Touch for Health* operates on this same invisible grid—using physical contact as a way to influence frequency flow.

Pairing muscle testing with frequency tools (like tuning forks or Tesla-inspired wave generators) adds another layer of coherence. Your hands become both listening devices and tuning instruments—scanning for distortion and applying resonance until the field responds.

This is the true alchemy of healing through touch: allowing the body to "hear" the right frequency and shift itself into harmony.

# PART III — TUNING & HEALING THE HUMAN FIELD

# Chapter 10: Tesla Frequencies & the Tuning of the Spine

*"If you want to find the secrets of the universe, think in terms of energy, frequency and vibration." – Nikola Tesla*

## Nervous System Alignment = Energetic Coherence

*Y*our spine is more than just a stack of bones holding you upright. It's the central highway of your nervous system—a conductor of electricity, energy, and subtle information.

When Tesla explored the nature of frequency, he intuitively grasped what modern biofield science now confirms: your body's energy systems rely on coherent electrical flow to regulate everything from digestion to thought clarity. Nowhere is this more evident than in the spine.

Every vertebra corresponds to key energetic centers, organs, and even emotional patterns. Misalignments—whether physical, emotional, or energetic—can disrupt the resonance along this axis, creating dissonance in the field. When we retune the spine, we don't just improve posture or relieve pain—we restore harmony across the entire energy system.

## The Spine as a Tuning Fork: Tesla's View Meets Energy Medicine

Tesla believed that each part of the universe vibrated at a unique frequency. Likewise, each vertebra along the spinal column resonates at a distinct frequency, both structurally and energetically. This concept provides the foundation for tuning fork therapy and other vibrational methods.

**When the spine is properly "tuned," your field becomes more coherent—meaning your thoughts, emotions, and body systems are working in rhythm.**

You can imagine your spine like the string of a musical instrument. Just as a guitar must be tuned to sound right, your spinal column must be vibrationally attuned to resonate with health, clarity, and higher states of awareness.

### Practical Tools for Tuning the Spine

Here are some hands-on methods that combine Tesla's principles with modern energy healing techniques:

### *Weighted Tuning Fork Protocol*

- **Use 128 Hz or 136.1 Hz forks** on spinal points, especially:
    - Occiput (base of the skull)
    - C7 (shoulders/neck junction)
    - T7 (diaphragm area)
    - L5/Sacrum (lower back/hip connection)

- **How to apply:**
  - Strike the tuning fork on a rubber activator.
  - Place the stem on the spinous process of each vertebra.
  - Hold for 10–20 seconds or until the vibration fades.

## Breath & Tone Realignment

- **Inhale deeply as you visualize energy rising up the spine.**
- **Exhale with a tone like "OM" or "AH" while touching or imagining each vertebra.**
- This stimulates vagus nerve tone and supports coherence.

## Micro-Movements + Intention

- Perform spinal waves or undulating motions from tailbone to crown.
- Combine movement with a specific affirmation or Tesla quote (e.g., "I am in tune with the frequency of healing.")

## Key Zones of Resonance

| Spinal Area | Energetic Impact | Tesla Frequency Tool |
|---|---|---|
| Cervical (C1–C7) | Mental clarity, communication | 528 Hz (DNA repair frequency) |
| Thoracic (T1–T12) | Emotional processing, heart & lungs | 417 Hz (transformation & release) |
| Lumbar (L1–L5) | Safety, grounding, digestion | 396 Hz (liberation from fear) |
| Sacrum/Coccyx | Ancestral patterns, base energy | 174 Hz (pain relief & grounding) |

## Why the Spine Responds to Frequency

The spinal cord and surrounding tissues are rich in water and collagen—both excellent conductors of vibrational information. When you introduce a pure, resonant frequency (like from a tuning fork), the vibration travels through the cerebrospinal fluid and fascia like ripples in a pond.

This creates a cascading recalibration effect, restoring both physical posture and energetic flow. Tesla's teachings remind us that *"resonance is the key to unlocking power."*

When your spine resonates, you *are* the power.

## Try This: The Tesla-Spine Tuning Ritual

1. Sit upright with spine aligned and relaxed.
2. Strike your tuning fork and place it gently on the crown of your head.
3. Close your eyes and *breathe deeply* as the sound travels down your spine.
4. Repeat the tone at the base of your skull, between shoulder blades, and sacrum.
5. Finish with three rounds of the mantra:
   **"I am aligned. I am in tune. I am energy."**

# Chapter 11: Tools of Coherence — Sound, Light, Magnetics, Intention

*W*hen your energy is scrambled, your thoughts foggy, or your emotions feel "off," it's usually a sign that coherence in your biofield has been disrupted. Coherence means harmony — a state where everything flows in sync. In Tesla's view, coherence was not just harmony of music or mechanics, but of **vibration** itself.

To restore this vibrational harmony, we can use tools that **entrain** the body — pulling our scattered energy back into order. These are not just gadgets; they are instruments of energetic intelligence.

### Sound as a Tuner of the Biofield

Sound affects energy instantly. A tuning fork placed near the body can realign frequencies, especially along the spine or over chakra points.

- **Weighted Tuning Forks**: Place on acupressure or spinal points to create physical vibration.
- **Unweighted Forks**: Use in the field around the body for clearing or energizing.

- **Chanting or Toning**: Use your own voice to hum, chant, or tone vowels. This self-generated sound is often the most coherent.

*Tesla Insight*: "If you want to find the secrets of the universe, think in terms of energy, frequency, and vibration."

## Light Therapy & Color Frequency

Each color corresponds to a frequency. Exposing your body or energy field to intentional light can rebalance systems.

- **Red Light Therapy**: Used to regenerate tissues and stimulate circulation.
- **Blue/Indigo Light**: Supports calming, insight, and sleep regulation.
- **Full-Spectrum or Color Filters**: Can be used in meditation, visualization, or targeted chakra support.

## Magnetics & Electromagnetism

Magnets and pulsed electromagnetic field (PEMF) therapy can influence cellular charge and nervous system balance.

- **Static Magnets**: Used over pain points or energy blockages.
- **PEMF Devices**: Send low-level pulses to support deep biofield alignment.
- **Tesla Coils or Scalar Devices**: Experimental but promising — said to open energy flow and re-pattern dissonance.

*Energetic Tip*: Always ground yourself before and after using electromagnetic devices.

## The Power of Intention

The most powerful tuning device is your consciousness.

- **Focus + Feeling = Frequency Shift**: Intention plus emotional charge creates coherence.
- **Heart-Brain Coherence Practices**: Sync heart rate and brain waves through breathing and gratitude.
- **Guided Visualization**: Direct energy like a current with focused mind imagery.

*Tesla meets Bioenergetics*: Tesla believed the brain was a receiver, not just a creator of thought. Intuition, intention, and higher mind states all rely on this energetic reception.

## Practitioner Application

- Begin each session with a *coherence reset*: breath, sound, and touch.
- Use **tuning forks** and **color filters** on specific zones from the Energeneic Blueprint™.
- Introduce **guided intention-setting** with clients to amplify healing.

# Tools of Coherence: Sound, Light, Magnetics, Intention

When it comes to healing and harmonizing the human energy field, *coherence* is the name of the game. Coherence is the state where all systems of the body—physical, emotional, mental, and energetic—are aligned and operating in harmony. And just as incoherence creates dis-ease, tools of coherence can guide the body back into balance.

These tools aren't new—many of them have ancient roots—but what's changed is our ability to understand and apply them with greater precision, thanks to Tesla-inspired science, frequency studies, and modern energetics.

## 1. Essential Oils

Aromatherapy is more than pleasant smells—it's vibrational medicine. Each plant carries a distinct energetic signature. When inhaled or applied to specific energy points, essential oils act as *emotional frequency harmonizers*. For example:

- **Lavender** calms and restores overactive frequencies (great for crown and heart coherence).
- **Peppermint** activates and invigorates blocked zones (especially helpful for the solar plexus and throat).
- **Frankincense** enhances spiritual alignment (third eye, crown, and auric field).

**Application Tip:** Use oils on acupressure points or chakras in combination with breath and intention for deeper results.

## 2. Tuning Forks

Tuning forks allow you to bring vibrational sound directly into the energy body. Each fork resonates at a specific frequency, acting like a tuning tool for "out-of-sync" parts of the system.

- **Weighted forks** are placed on physical points (spine, joints, chakras).
- **Unweighted forks** are used around the auric field to clear static and restore flow.

**Tesla Tip:** Use a 528 Hz tuning fork along the spine to stimulate the heart field and cellular repair frequencies.

## 3. Color Frequencies

Color is simply light vibrating at different frequencies. You can "bathe" energy centers in the light they need:

- **Red** for grounding and activating the root
- **Yellow** for digestion, willpower, and clearing the mental field
- **Indigo** for intuition, vision, and recalibrating the third eye

**Tech Tip:** Use colored light wands, bio-resonance lamps, or even colored silk cloths in healing spaces.

### 4. Scalar & Magnetic Therapy

Scalar energy (zero-point energy) is the subtle field Tesla explored that exists beyond measurable EMF. When delivered through scalar-emitting tools, this energy can promote deep coherence, regeneration, and alignment.

Magnetic therapy, on the other hand, uses north/south polarity to encourage better circulation, inflammation relief, and energetic realignment.

### Devices may include:

- Scalar pendants or plates
- PEMF mats (Pulsed Electromagnetic Field)
- Biofield-enhancing magnets applied to acupuncture zones

### 5. Intention

Perhaps the most powerful coherence tool of all is *conscious intention*. Intention acts as the steering wheel for energy. When combined with sound, touch, scent, or light, it amplifies healing exponentially.

**Practice Tip:** Before every session, set an intention out loud or in thought. Example: "This energy will clear, align, and restore the highest frequency of joy and vitality."

Together, these tools form the *Tesla-Inspired Coherence Kit*—a non-invasive, powerful way to tune the human biofield back to its natural harmonic state.

# Chapter 12: The Daily Reset — Grounding, Breathing, Aligning

*I*n a world that pulls your energy in every direction, the Daily Reset is your energetic anchor. It's a simple, repeatable set of tools that restore coherence, re-establish your energetic alignment, and give your body a fresh start—anytime, anywhere.

## Why a Daily Reset?

Your energetic field is affected by:

- Environmental noise (EMFs, toxins, stress)
- Emotional residue (yours or others')
- Mental loops and unresolved tension
- Physical postural imbalances

Just like brushing your teeth clears debris from the mouth, the Daily Reset clears energetic "plaque" from your field. The more consistently you reset, the easier it is to stay in your coherent zone.

## Three Pillars of the Daily Reset

 *1. Grounding: Anchor to the Earth*

Grounding re-establishes your connection to the planet's stabilizing energy field, which naturally helps drain excess charge or static from your system.

### Quick Protocol: Barefoot Grounding + Root Breath

- Stand or sit with bare feet on the earth (grass, sand, soil).
- Inhale deeply through the nose, feeling the breath fill your belly.
- On exhale, imagine any tension draining through your feet into the ground.
- Repeat for 3–5 minutes.

**Add Tesla Layer**: Visualize yourself connected to the Earth like a grounded wire—discharging static and receiving replenishing magnetic waves.

 *2. Breathing: Reset the Rhythm*

Your breath is your built-in frequency tuner. When shallow or erratic, the body loses coherence. When rhythmic and deep, it restores harmony between heart, brain, and energy field.

### Quick Protocol: Coherence Breath

- Inhale for 5 seconds, exhale for 5 seconds.
- Repeat for 2–5 minutes.
- Place one hand over your heart, the other over your belly.

- Visualize a wave of light rising and falling as you breathe.

**Tip**: Try this while listening to 432 Hz or 528 Hz music to amplify coherence.

 *3. Aligning: Reconnect Vertical Flow*

Energy moves vertically through the body from root to crown. Misalignment in posture or intention kinks the flow. Realignment reopens your main energetic channels.

### Quick Protocol: The Energetic Zipline

- Stand or sit tall. Imagine a golden cord from the top of your head to the base of your spine.
- As you breathe in, picture energy flowing up from the earth to your crown.
- As you breathe out, see energy cascading back down, rinsing your system.
- Repeat while humming softly to activate vibrational flow.

### Sample Practitioner Reset (10 Minutes)

Use this routine at the start of each session—or as a personal daily practice:

1. **Ground**: 2 min barefoot + breath
2. **Breathe**: 2 min coherence breath + heart focus
3. **Align**: 3 min golden zipline + tone (hum "Om" or your chosen mantra)
4. **Seal**: 3 min oil anointment or magnetic comb sweep down the field

## Optional Tools to Enhance Reset

- **Essential Oils**: Vetiver (grounding), Frankincense (alignment), Citrus (clarity)
- **Tuning Forks**: 136.1 Hz for grounding; 528 Hz for coherence
- **Color Light**: Red for root, green for heart, violet for crown

# Chapter 13: Mapping the Path to Energetic Integrity

*What alignment feels like — and how to recognize (and correct) energetic distortion*

## What Is Energetic Integrity?

$\mathcal{E}$nergetic integrity is the state in which your physical body, emotional body, mental field, and soul essence are operating in harmony. It's when your outer actions reflect your inner truth. You feel "plugged in," clear-headed, emotionally balanced, and connected to purpose.

Think of it like tuning a symphony. When all instruments (your body systems) are in tune, the music flows. When one is off—even slightly—the dissonance can be felt, even if it's subtle at first.

**What Is Energetic Integrity?**

Energetic integrity is the full coherence between:

- The **Physical Body** (cellular health, somatic tension, posture, strength)
- The **Emotional Body** (unprocessed feelings, reactive patterns, hormonal signals)
- The **Mental Field** (thoughts, beliefs, intentions, inner narratives)

- The **Soul Essence** (your divine code, life purpose, higher connection)

When these are harmonized, energy flows like a circuit without interference. You become a living Tesla coil—radiating clean, purposeful frequency.

## What Alignment *Feels* Like

When you're in energetic alignment:

- Your thoughts are clear, and decisions feel easy.
- Emotions flow without overwhelm or suppression.
- Physical energy is steady—not manic or depleted.
- You feel a subtle "rightness" in your core.
- There's an inner spaciousness or flow—like a river unblocked.
- Synchronicities tend to increase.
- You feel more present in your body and less reactive to chaos around you.

## Signs You're Out of Alignment

Just as pain is a signal in the body, energetic distortion sends cues:

- You feel "off" without knowing why.
- You're fatigued even after sleep.
- Repetitive thoughts cycle without resolution.
- Your body feels heavy, tense, or disconnected.
- Emotional "stickiness"—like you can't shake a mood.
- Constant external friction (things going wrong).
- You lose your sense of joy, clarity, or direction.

## How to Correct Energetic Misalignment

The Energeneic Method offers several techniques for restoring coherence:

 **1. BIOFIELD MAPPING CHECK-IN**

In the Tesla-inspired Energeneic Method, **Biofield Mapping** is your diagnostic compass—a sensory scan of the human energy field designed to detect distortion before it crystallizes into dysfunction.

Use your Energeneic Mapping skills to scan zones for depletion, overactivity, or blockages. Pay attention to areas of physical discomfort, tingling, or numbness. These are often entry points for release.

Think of your energy body like a dynamic electromagnetic system—just as Tesla believed all matter vibrates, your biofield communicates in frequency signatures. When something is "off," the field doesn't lie. This is your signal to tune in.

Begin by scanning the body from head to toe, using hand sensitivity, a pendulum, or muscle testing. Move slowly over each zone, observing for fluctuations in sensation, temperature, or pressure. You are not looking for the obvious—you are listening for the **whisper of imbalance**.

**What to Identify:**

- **Depletion**
  Areas that feel hollow, cool, or energetically vacant—often tied to chronic fatigue, numbness, or low mood.
- **Congestion**
  Zones that feel hot, sticky, overly dense, or emotionally chaotic—frequently linked to inflammation, looping thoughts, or anxious tension.
- **Blockage**
  Locations where the signal simply drops—no feedback, no flow. This may indicate trauma storage, emotional shutdown, or energetic protection mechanisms.

Subtle ripples in the field—like pulsing, collapse, or static—are clues pointing toward **energetic disharmony**. Treat these not as malfunctions, but as messages—your field is asking to be witnessed, not silenced.

## What Is Depletion in Your Energy Field?

**Depletion** is like a low battery inside your body's energy system.

Imagine you have an invisible bubble around you—your *biofield*—and certain parts of it are running out of power. These places might feel:

- **Empty or hollow** — like something is missing.
- **Cool or cold** to the touch — even if the rest of your body feels warm.
- **Numb or dull** — you can't feel much sensation there.
- **Tired or down** — emotions feel flat, heavy, or hopeless.

This often shows up when someone feels **drained**, like they can't get going no matter how much they rest. It's common in people who've been sick for a long time, are burned out, or feel sad without knowing why.

### How to Find Depletion Areas

You don't need to "see energy" to spot this—use your **hands and awareness**.

1. **Rub your hands together** for a few seconds to activate energy sensitivity.
2. Slowly **scan over your body** (or someone else's) with your palms, starting at the head and moving down.
3. Pay attention: Does any area feel **empty, cold, or blank**? That's likely a depleted zone.
4. You can also try a **pendulum** or **muscle testing** to check for weak spots.

**Common places** where people get depleted: lower back, chest, belly, and knees—anywhere you've had pain or tension for a while.

### How to Refill Depleted Zones

Think of it like charging your phone—but with energy instead of electricity.

Try this:

- **Breathe** slowly into the depleted spot. Imagine golden light filling it up like warm sunshine.
- **Hum a sound** you like while touching the area. Sound wakes it up gently.
- **Tap or massage lightly** with your fingers—this helps wake up the nerves and invite circulation.

- **Place your hand there with loving attention**.
  Reiki, magnetics, or visualization all help.

Most importantly, **rest and kindness** are part of healing. Your body isn't broken—it's just asking for care.

## Congestion: When Your Energy Gets "Stuck in Traffic"

Imagine your energy field like a network of highways made of light and vibration. When everything's flowing well, it's like traffic moving smoothly—everyone gets where they need to go. But sometimes, things jam up.

That jam? That's **congestion.**

It's when too much energy piles up in one area and can't move freely.

*What It Feels Like*

- That spot might feel **hot** or **tight** to the touch.
- You might sense a **buzzing**, **stickiness**, or like the area is "overfull."
- It can feel like there's emotional **chaos** or noise in that zone—like your body is shouting at you.
- It often shows up with:
  - **Inflammation** (swelling, redness)
  - **Overthinking** or racing thoughts
  - **Anxiety or restlessness**

You're not broken—your body is just trying to get your attention.

*How to Work With Congestion (Tesla Style)*

Using your **Energeneic Mapping** tools, you can help your body restore flow:

## 1. Scan for Congestion

Use your hand (like a sensor), a pendulum, or muscle testing. Move slowly over your body from head to toe.

- Congested areas often feel **warmer**, **stickier**, or like the energy "pushes back."
- Trust what you sense, even if it feels subtle.

**Tip**: Think of it like a Tesla coil detecting energy pressure points.

## 2. Release the Pressure With the Coherence Triad

**Breath**: Try **4–7–8 breathing**:

- Inhale for 4 seconds
- Hold for 7
- Exhale for 8 (add a soft hum on the exhale to break up dense energy)

**Tone**: Make a sound that matches how your body feels. It could be a "mmmm," "ahhh," or even a low hum. The vibration helps break up energetic clumps.

**Touch**: Gently tap or massage key points:

- **K27 (collarbone points)** to reset the nervous system.
- **Solar plexus** or **heart center** to clear emotional tension.
- **Sacral** if emotions feel stuck in the belly.

### 3. Emotional Decoder Ring

Ask the congestion:

- "What emotion is stuck here?"
- "Is there something I'm not allowing myself to feel?"
- "What would help this energy move?"

Sometimes the congestion is old stress, grief, or pressure trying to be heard. Just acknowledging it can start the release.

### 4. Move It, Don't Fight It

Congested energy wants to move. After breath and touch:

- **Stretch gently** or do a simple flow movement.
- Play **low-frequency music** (like 528Hz or Solfeggio tones).
- Add a drop of peppermint or eucalyptus oil (if you have some) to open the flow.

Bonus Tesla Tip: Imagine the area pulsing with bright electric-blue light—shaking loose what no longer serves you.

## Blockage

**What It Feels Like:**
Blockages in your energy field are like dead zones—places where the energy just doesn't move. If your biofield were a river, this is where the water isn't flowing at all. These zones may feel totally numb, super resistant, or even invisible to your awareness—like your hand passes over and "feels nothing."

**Common Clues:**

- You try to focus on or connect with the area, but it feels... gone.
- No heat, no sensation—just blank.
- You might feel frustrated, zoned out, or emotionally "shut down" when attention moves to this part of the body or field.
- These spots can be linked to emotional trauma, deep fear, or repressed experiences.

## How to Work With a Blockage

1. **Think of It Like an Energy Blackout**
   Just like your Wi-Fi might cut out when there's interference, your energy can stop flowing in a certain zone. You're not broken—you just need to gently reconnect the signal.
2. **Try the "Signal Tap" Test**
   Lightly tap or brush your fingers in a circle over the blocked area. Feel nothing? That's your clue. Try humming as you do it (yep, seriously—it helps vibration move). Pay attention to where sensation "comes back."
3. **Name It to Claim It**
   Quietly ask:
   *"Is there something you're hiding here?"*
   *"What part of me did I turn off?"*
   You don't have to get a big answer—just be curious. A word, color, or feeling might pop up.
4. **Reboot With Breath + Touch**
   - Breathe slowly into the area (even if you can't feel it).
   - Place your palm over it and imagine light slowly filling the spot.
   - Say out loud: *"It's safe for energy to move here again."*

5. **Small Shifts Matter**
   Blockages might not open in one try. It's okay.
   Even feeling tingles, heat, or emotion come up
   later in the day means the system is rebooting.

**Tesla Insight:**
Nikola Tesla believed that all energy is vibration. When a
part of your field goes "off the grid," your job isn't to
force it—but to *tune it*. Think of yourself like a human
radio, adjusting the dial until the signal returns.

 **2. THE COHERENCE TRIAD**

Activate the **Breath – Tone – Touch** sequence:

- **Breath**: Try a 4–7–8 reset or vertical box breath
  through the spine.
- **Tone**: Hum or tone on the exhale. Choose the
  note your body craves.
- **Touch**: Lightly tap or massage key meridian or
  chakra points (e.g., K27, heart center, sacral).

**The Coherence Triad: Breath – Tone – Touch**

When your energy feels off, this simple three-part method
helps bring your system back into balance—like hitting a
reset button for your body, mind, and soul.

*1. Breath – The Power of Rhythmic Breathing*

Breath is your fastest way to shift your state.

**Try This: The 4–7–8 Breath**

- Sit or lie down somewhere quiet.
- Inhale gently through your nose for **4 seconds**.

- Hold that breath for **7 seconds**.
- Exhale slowly through your mouth for **8 seconds**.
- Repeat this cycle **4 times**.

Why it works: This breath pattern relaxes your nervous system, calms racing thoughts, and stabilizes your energy field. It's especially good if you're feeling anxious or "jangly" inside.

## Alternate Option: Vertical Box Breath

- Imagine your breath flowing up and down your spine.
- Inhale up the spine to the crown of your head (4 counts).
- Hold it at the top (4 counts).
- Exhale down the spine to the base (4 counts).
- Hold at the bottom (4 counts).
- Repeat in a slow, steady rhythm for 1–2 minutes.

*This type of breath aligns your spine with your energy field like tuning a central column of light.*

## 2. Tone – Humming to Heal

Your voice is a built-in tuning fork.

## Try This: Tonal Reset

- After a breath cycle, take a deep inhale.
- As you exhale, **hum** gently—like "mmmmmm"— and notice where you feel it in your body.
- You can try different sounds like:
  - **"Ohhhh"** (opens the heart)
  - **"Ahhhh"** (good for stress)
  - **"Eeeeee"** (clears the head and crown)

**Tip:** Try a few and choose the one your body *likes best.* That's the frequency you need most.

Why it works: Humming sends vibration through your bones and tissues, shifting stuck energy and stimulating the vagus nerve—your body's calming switch.

### *3. Touch – Hands-on Energy Reset*

Now anchor it physically with gentle touch.

### Try This: Meridian & Chakra Activation

- **K27 Points:** Find the little dips below your collarbones (where a backpack strap would sit). Tap or massage them gently for 10–15 seconds. This clears mental fog.
- **Heart Center:** Place your hand in the middle of your chest and gently rub in small circles. It opens emotional flow.
- **Sacral Area:** Rest your hand below your belly button. Breathe here for grounding and emotional ease.

*Bonus: If you're using tools like magnets, crystals, or essential oils, this is the time to add them.*

### Putting It All Together

1. **Sit quietly** and check in: How does your energy feel?
2. **Do 4 rounds of 4–7–8 breathing** or vertical spine breathing.
3. **Add a few minutes of toning**, letting your body guide the sounds.
4. **Touch or tap your energy points** to anchor the reset.
5. **Pause and feel:** What's changed?

Even doing this for just **5 minutes a day** can rewire how your energy flows—and help you correct distortion before it causes deeper issues.

 **3. EMOTIONAL INQUIRY**

Ask:

"What am I not expressing?"
"What frequency is stuck here?"
"What would bring flow?"

This helps decode stuck energy before it manifests physically.

### Step 3: Emotional Inquiry – How to Ask & Decode Stuck Energy

Energy doesn't just get stuck physically—it also holds **emotions**. These emotional "frequencies" can become trapped in different areas of your body, especially if you suppress feelings like anger, fear, grief, or shame. This step teaches you how to listen inward and **ask your body** what it's trying to tell you—before it turns into pain or illness.

WHY IT MATTERS

If you skip this step, you might only treat the symptom, not the **root cause**. Emotions are energy in motion—when they don't move, they stagnate, just like water in a blocked pipe.

HOW-TO: 3 Questions That Open the Flow

Find a quiet space. Sit or lie down. After doing Breath–Tone–Touch (Step 2), gently place your hand over the area of congestion, blockage, or depletion. Then ask these questions—either aloud or silently.

### 1. "What am I not expressing?"

*This helps identify suppressed emotion.*

- If you feel tightness in your throat: "Am I not speaking my truth?"
- In the belly: "Am I holding onto fear or nervousness?"
- In the chest: "Am I not letting myself feel sadness or love?"

**Tip**: Don't judge the answer. It may come as a word, a memory, a color, a body sensation, or even a tear.

### 2. "What frequency is stuck here?"

*This question reveals the "vibe" or emotional tone—anger, guilt, shame, grief, etc.*

- Imagine tuning a radio. Ask: "Is this grief? Shame? Rage? Fear? Regret?"
- Listen for what your body "tunes into."

**Beginner tip**: Don't overthink. Just go with the first feeling or word that pops into your mind.

### 3. "What would bring flow?"

*This is the healing prompt. It invites action or shift.*

- Maybe your body wants to stretch, cry, dance, breathe deeply, or even laugh.
- Maybe it wants forgiveness, expression, or just silence.

**Let your body answer.** Often, it already knows what would help—if you just listen.

### What to Do With the Answers

- **Write them in a journal.**
- **Do energy work** (like Reiki or touch) on the area while holding the feeling.
- **Visualize release**—like light flowing into the space and carrying the stuck feeling away.
- **Say it aloud**: "I give this feeling permission to move."

This Emotional Inquiry practice works best when you're **present, gentle, and honest**. It's not about fixing yourself—it's about listening deeply so your energy can **self-correct**, the way Tesla believed energy does when brought into harmonic resonance.

## 4. REALIGNMENT RITUAL

Use your personalized Energeneic Daily Reset:

- Ground → Breathe → Map → Intend → Realign
- Consider adding oils, sound, or magnetics as needed.

### Use your personalized Energeneic Daily Reset

This daily practice is designed to realign your energy field, stabilize your emotions, and reconnect you to Source. It's like brushing your teeth—but for your energy system.

### *Step 1: Ground*

**Why:** Before you do any energy work, you must be present in your body. Grounding connects you to the Earth's stabilizing field.

### How-To:

- Stand or sit with feet flat on the floor.
- Imagine roots growing from the soles of your feet deep into the earth.
- Say aloud or silently: *"I am grounded. I am safe. I am supported."*
- Optional: Hold a grounding crystal (e.g., hematite or black tourmaline) or step outdoors barefoot for 2–5 minutes.

### *Step 2: Breathe*

**Why:** Breath is the bridge between body and spirit. Specific breathwork clears mental fog and resets your nervous system.

## How-To Options:

- **4–7–8 Breath Reset:** Inhale for 4 seconds, hold for 7, exhale for 8. Repeat 3–5 times.
- **Vertical Box Breath (Spinal Flow):**
    1. Inhale up the spine (root to crown) for 4 counts.
    2. Hold at the top (crown) for 4 counts.
    3. Exhale down the spine (crown to root) for 4 counts.
    4. Hold at the base for 4 counts.
       Repeat for 4 cycles.

### Step 3: Map

**Why:** Awareness precedes healing. Mapping helps you locate energetic congestion, depletion, or blockages.

### How-To:

- Close your eyes and scan your body slowly from head to toe.
- Use your hand, a pendulum, or your intuition.
- Ask: *Where feels off? Where is tight, hot, empty, numb, or overactive?*
- Gently place your hand or attention on those areas for the next steps.

### Step 4: Intend

**Why:** Intention directs energy. By setting a clear focus, your system knows what to shift.

### How-To:

- Place your hand over a mapped area or chakra.
- Say:
    o *"I invite balance and flow here."*

- o  *"I release what no longer serves."*
- o  *"I realign with vitality, peace, and clarity."*
- Use a tone or hum that resonates in that area. Trust the note your body wants to release.

### Step 5: Realign

**Why:** This is where transformation happens—through vibration, sensory tools, and body awareness.

### How-To (choose 1–3 of these add-ons):

- **Essential Oils:** Rub grounding (e.g., vetiver), uplifting (e.g., orange), or balancing (e.g., lavender) oils into mapped areas.
- **Tuning Forks or Singing Bowls:** Apply sound to blocked or depleted zones. Let vibration do the work.
- **Magnets or PEMF:** Place gentle energy devices on the mapped zones to restore harmony.
- **Tapping or Gentle Massage:** Use fingers or tools (e.g., gua sha, reflexology wand) to activate meridian or chakra points (K27, heart, sacral, etc.).
- **Visualization:** See your entire aura as a glowing, pulsing light—smooth, whole, flowing.

### Suggested Affirmation to Close:

*"I am clear. I am aligned. I am energetically whole."*

Do this ritual daily—or anytime your system feels "off"—to build energetic resilience and clarity.

## TESLA-INSPIRED MAGNETIC TOOLS FOR ENERGY ALIGNMENT

Magnets, when used thoughtfully, can support energy flow, restore polarity, and amplify biofield coherence. These tools are not about brute force, but subtle influence—aligning the natural magnetic blueprint of your body with Earth's electromagnetic rhythm.

Below are some advanced but beginner-accessible magnetic tools inspired by Tesla's ideas and modern bioenergetics:

### 1. Polarity-Tested Neodymium Discs

**What it is:** Small but strong rare-earth magnets with marked poles (North/South).
**How to use:**

- **Locate the area of depletion or blockage** via muscle testing, pendulum dowsing, or hand scanning.
- **North pole side (cooling, calming)** faces the skin for inflammation or hyperactivity.
- **South pole side (energizing, warming)** faces the skin for fatigue, coldness, or low energy.
- **Duration:** 5–20 minutes per session. Place gently and tape down if needed.

### Common placements:

- Over the **solar plexus** (digestive balance)
- On **wrists or ankles** (meridian stimulation)
- Along the **spine** (nervous system harmonizing)

## 2. Bipolar Magnetic Foot Insoles

**What it is:** Insoles with alternating North/South poles embedded throughout.
**How to use:**

- Insert into shoes and **wear during walking, yoga, or grounding rituals**.
- Stimulates the **Kidney 1 point (Yongquan)** and helps **pull energy down** from an overactive mind.
- Ideal for those with anxiety, ungroundedness, or poor circulation.

**Pro tip:** Use barefoot on a grounding mat with these insoles to layer magnetic and Earth energy.

## 3. Magnetic Roller Wand

**What it is:** A handheld device with rolling magnetic balls or discs.
**How to use:**

- Roll gently along **meridians** (e.g., bladder line on the back, stomach line on legs).
- Combine with **acupressure or reflexology charts** for precise targeting.
- Use in **figure-8 motions** for brain balancing (e.g., across forehead or arms).

**When to use:** During energy balancing routines, after emotional releases, or pre-bedtime.

### 4. Tesla Coil + Magnet Combo

**What it is:** A Tesla coil that emits low-level high-frequency energy, used alongside static magnets for field amplification.

**How to use:**

- **Place Tesla coil nearby** (not on the body) to create a resonant energy field.
- **Apply magnets on the body** while Tesla coil pulses.
- **Focus intention on realignment or regeneration.**
- Use in a quiet space for **10–15 minutes** max when starting.

**Caution:** Always read device safety instructions. Not suitable for people with pacemakers or epilepsy.

### Choosing the Right Tool

Ask yourself:

- Am I trying to **stimulate energy** (South pole, active magnets)?
- Do I need to **calm or reduce heat** (North pole, calming placement)?
- Is the issue **deep or shallow** (foot insoles = daily support; roller = targeted; coil = field-wide)?

Start simple, and document your response in a **biofield journal** to track outcomes.

## HOW DO MAGNETS WORK IN ENERGY MEDICINE?

The body is electric and magnetic—your heart, brain, and cells all emit measurable bioelectromagnetic fields.

Magnets are believed to influence:

- **Ionic exchange** in cells (supporting detox and healing)
- **Energy flow** through the meridians or chakra system
- **Polarity correction** when parts of the field are reversed, sluggish, or congested

Tesla's coil amplified electrical current; in parallel, healing magnets help **redirect and stabilize the body's energetic current.**

## Types of Magnets Used in Healing

| Type | Field Strength | Common Uses |
|---|---|---|
| **Neodymium** | High | Spot treatment, acupoints, meridians |
| **Ceramic** | Medium | Wearable magnets (bracelets, soles) |
| **Bipolar pairs** | High | For magnet pair therapy (e.g. biomagnetism) |
| **Magnetic mats** | Low to medium | Full-body balancing |

## Polarity Basics: North vs. South Pole

- **North Pole (-):** Sedates, calms, cools inflammation, used for pain relief
- **South Pole (+):** Stimulates, energizes, used for regeneration or chronic fatigue

**Important:** Never apply strong south pole magnets over tumors or acute inflammation, as it may overstimulate growth or heat.

## Common Healing Applications

*1. Chakra Balancing*

- Place a **south pole** magnet 2–3 inches above underactive chakras.
- Use **north pole** magnets for calming overstimulated chakras.

*2. Pain and Inflammation Relief*

- Apply **north pole** magnet directly over painful joint, muscle, or tendon.
- Use for 15–30 minutes, 1–3 times per day.

*3. Energy Realignment (Tesla Method)*

- Place magnets along the **spine (Governing Vessel meridian)** to reset energetic flow.
- Alternate polarity (North-South-North) to pulse the field gently.

*4. Meridian Tracing*

- Use a **magnet wand** to trace meridian pathways.
- Helpful for removing blockages or congestion, especially with toning/breathwork.

*5. EMF Detox / Reset*

- Place magnets at:
  - **Base of skull (GB20)**
  - **Heart center**
  - **Root chakra**
- Combine with breath → tone → touch to recalibrate the biofield.

## Tesla-Inspired Biofield Use

In your *Tesla's Code* framework, magnets can serve as:

- **Frequency stabilizers** after breath and tone sessions
- **Field amplifiers** when placed near Tesla coils or PEMF pads
- **Energy anchors** to hold intention during Energeneic Mapping or Realignment

Magnets aren't the source of healing—they simply help **the body's innate intelligence** reorganize its energy more efficiently.

## Safety Guidelines

- **Do not use** magnets over:
  - Pacemakers or electronic implants
  - Open wounds or active bleeding
  - Pregnant abdomen (use only under trained supervision)
  - Tumors unless polarity is professionally assessed
- Limit **session times** (15–30 min) until you know how the body responds.
- Always start with **lower strength magnets** before using high-powered neodymium.

## Not Everyone Should Use Magnet Tools: Safety Guidelines & Contraindications

While magnetic therapy tools can be powerful allies in bioenergetic realignment, **they're not universally safe or suitable for all individuals**. The body's energy system is sensitive, and in some people—especially those with unique neurological, cardiac, or energetic profiles—**magnetic fields may overstimulate, dysregulate, or interfere** with natural balance or medical equipment.

### Who Should Avoid Magnetic Therapy?

1. **Individuals with Pacemakers or Implanted Devices**
   Magnets can **disrupt the functioning of pacemakers, defibrillators, insulin pumps**, and other implanted devices. Strong neodymium magnets especially can pose serious risks.
2. **Pregnant Women**
   Due to the sensitive nature of developing fetal tissue and lack of safety research, magnetic therapy is generally **not recommended during pregnancy**.
3. **People with Seizure Disorders or Epilepsy**
   Magnetic fields may affect **neuronal firing and electromagnetic thresholds**, potentially triggering neurological events in sensitive individuals.
4. **Children under 7 years old**
   Children's energetic systems are **still forming and more vulnerable** to artificial energy manipulation. Use only under the guidance of a trained energy therapist.
5. **Highly Sensitive Individuals (HSPs, empaths, or those with energy hypersensitivity)**
   Some people report **nausea, dizziness, headaches, emotional flooding**, or extreme

fatigue when exposed to magnetic fields—even mild ones.
6.  Tumors and Magnetic Fields: A Special Caution

Magnetic therapy should **not be applied directly over tumors or cancerous areas** unless the **polarity, strength, and positioning of the magnets are professionally assessed and overseen by a qualified healthcare provider** experienced in bioenergetics or oncology-informed energy medicine.

Here's why:

- **Unclear Effects on Cellular Growth:** Magnets can influence cellular ion channels and electromagnetic signaling. While this can stimulate healing in healthy tissue, there is concern that inappropriate application—especially of **north (negative) polarity or strong static fields**—may inadvertently stimulate blood flow or cell activity near tumor sites.
- **Lack of Clinical Consensus:** There is **insufficient large-scale clinical evidence** to establish that magnets are safe or beneficial in the presence of tumors. Some case reports suggest possible stimulation of tumor growth or lymphatic spread when magnets are misused.
- **Energetic Complexity of Tumors:** From a Tesla-inspired or Energeneic lens, tumors are not simply physical masses—they are **energetic distortions**, often resulting from unresolved emotional frequency patterns, environmental toxins, and biofield chaos. Directly applying magnetic force to a distortion can further confuse the system unless extremely nuanced.

### *How to Gauge Magnetic Sensitivity (Self-Test)*

Before using any magnetic device:

1. **Start with very low exposure** (e.g., place a low-strength magnet 2–3 inches from the skin).
2. Tune in to your body for 1–2 minutes. Do you feel **tingling, pulsing, heat, agitation, dizziness, or anxiety**?
3. Remove the magnet and wait. If symptoms subside, you may be sensitive.
4. For safe exploration, use **muscle testing, a pendulum**, or **energetic mapping** to confirm suitability.

### *Tips for Safe Magnetic Use*

- Always **start short and low**: 1–3 minutes on low areas (e.g., feet or lower back).
- Avoid placing magnets **directly on the heart, brain, thyroid, or reproductive** organs unless guided by a trained practitioner.
- Combine with **grounding techniques** (barefoot outside, deep breathing) to stabilize.
- **Rotate tools**—don't overuse one device or spot.
- Take breaks: Overuse can cause **energetic whiplash or detox reactions** (headache, fatigue, mood swings).

### *Why Limit Magnet Therapy Duration?*

The human biofield can be **highly sensitive to electromagnetic stimulation**, and not everyone responds the same way. Limiting initial exposure allows:

- **Your body to adapt gradually** to the shift in polarity and field amplitude.

- **Your nervous system to remain balanced**, preventing overstimulation (such as dizziness, fatigue, or agitation).
- **Clear observation of effects**, so you can track positive changes—or early signs of intolerance.

## *How to Start Safe Sessions*

1. **Start with 15 minutes max**—especially if you're new to biofield tools.
2. **Position carefully**: Use only on one localized area at a time (e.g., a knee, back, or foot).
3. **Notice reactions**: Track changes in warmth, tingling, mood, or energy afterward.
4. **Wait 24 hours** before repeating in the same spot.
5. **Gradually increase** to 30 minutes if you feel well-regulated and grounded after a few sessions.

## *Add Grounding After*

To rebalance after a magnetic session, follow up with:

- Hydration (add minerals or electrolytes)
- Barefoot contact with the earth (if possible)
- Slow, mindful breathing (to integrate shifts)

## Always Start Low and Go Slow

### *Why This Matters:*

Neodymium magnets are incredibly powerful—even the small ones. Using high-strength magnets (especially over 1000 Gauss) too soon can overstimulate the nervous system or disrupt the natural flow of energy, especially in sensitive individuals. Symptoms might include fatigue, dizziness, nausea, or emotional agitation.

*How to Begin:*

1. **Choose a Low-Gauss Magnet First:**
   - Start with magnets rated **200–800 Gauss** (mild therapeutic level).
   - Examples: magnetic bracelets, small flat discs, magnetic insoles.

2. **Use Brief Exposure:**
   - Begin with **5–10 minute sessions**, once per day.
   - Observe for any reactions (fatigue, tingling, energy spikes/drops).

3. **Gradually Increase Duration:**
   - If no discomfort arises, extend to 15–20 minutes over several days or weeks.

4. **Test Polarity Placement:**
   - North pole (negative) typically has a calming, sedating effect.
   - South pole (positive) tends to energize or stimulate.
   - Test one side at a time—never both at once unless trained.

5. **Progress Cautiously to Stronger Tools:**
   - Once tolerance is built, introduce higher Gauss magnets like **bipolar insoles**, **roller wands**, or **magnetic mattress pads**.

*Energetic Check-In:*

Before and after each session, perform a **Biofield Mapping Scan** (head to toe) to assess changes:

- Did the area feel more open or grounded?
- Any new sensations or emotions emerge?
- Was there a noticeable shift in breath, temperature, or mood?

## How to Verify Magnet Tools: Polarity, Authenticity & Gauss Rating

*1. Verify Polarity (North vs South Pole)*

- Use a standard compass: move one end of the magnet close to the compass needle. The end of your magnet that attracts the **south-pointing (usually blue or white) end of the compass needle** is the **north pole** of the magnet.
- Alternatively, you can suspend the magnet on a thin string so it can rotate freely. When it stops, the end pointing toward geographic north is the magnet's **north pole**.
- Many therapeutic magnets are marked "N" (north pole) or "S" (south pole). Make sure the markings match the vendor's specifications.

*2. Check Authenticity & Grade*

- Many magnets are marketed with high grades (e.g., N52 for neodymium) but may not deliver the claimed strength. To check authenticity:
  - Use a simple "lift test": measure how much weight the magnet can lift compared to the advertised grade.
  - Compare the magnet's pull force or measured flux against known values for that size/grade.
  - Check the vendor's datasheet or certificate of authenticity. If none is provided, consider it a risk.

*3. Measure Gauss Rating (Magnetic Field Strength)*

- A Gaussmeter measures the magnetic flux density of a magnet (in gauss or tesla).
- To use:
  - o Position the probe of the gaussmeter close to, or on the surface of, the magnet. Closer = stronger reading.
  - o Refer to manufacturer specs: if the magnet claims e.g., 3000 Gs (0.3 T), your measurement should be close. Significant deviation suggests weaker or fake magnet.
- Note: Measurement depends on magnet size, shape, surface, and distance. Use a consistent method.

*4. Best Practice Timeline*

- Before first use: verify polarity and measure gauss in a quiet, stable environment.
- Keep a record (photo of meter reading, date, magnet details).
- After purchase, use magnet at low strength and short duration (e.g., 5-10 min), then monitor how the body responds.
- If results are weak or body reacts negatively, reassess tool, vendor, or use.

*5. Why This Matters for Your Energeneic Practice*

- Proper polarity ensures you apply the **correct energetic effect** (calming vs stimulating).
- Authentic grade ensures you're working within predictable energetic parameters—especially important for safety and reproducibility.
- Measuring gauss helps you integrate magnets as tools rather than guessing—they become part of your energetic protocol with integrity.

# Becoming a Tesla-Style Healer: Ethics & Responsibility

### The Foundation of Integrity

To work with Tesla-style energy tools—be it frequencies, magnets, or subtle energy—you are stepping into the role of an energetic steward. This work amplifies not just power, but *intention*. Therefore, ethical clarity is not optional—it's vital.

Ask yourself often:

- Am I using this energy with full consent?
- Am I tuning into the client's highest good, or imposing my vision?
- Would I feel at peace if my healing work were made visible to the world?

Integrity means staying aligned with your values and not compromising energetic responsibility for fame, ego, or profit.

### Setting Clear Boundaries

Energy work is intimate. It involves invisible dynamics that can blur emotional, spiritual, and physical boundaries if not addressed clearly.

- **Energetic hygiene:** Clear your field *before and after* each session.
- **Professional scope:** Know your limits. Tesla-style healing is powerful, but it's not a replacement for medical diagnosis or psychological counseling.

- **Client autonomy:** Always receive informed consent, explain what tools you're using, and *never* override the client's inner wisdom.

*Remember: The more powerful the tool, the more disciplined the operator must be.*

## The New Paradigm of Care

Tesla was ahead of his time—and so are you. The emerging paradigm is not about fixing others, but about:

- **Coherence over control**
- **Vibration over manipulation**
- **Collaboration over hierarchy**

You're not the healer—you're the *frequency tuner*. The body, soul, and field of the client do the healing. You simply create the conditions.

Key mindset shifts:

| Old Paradigm | Tesla-Style Paradigm |
| --- | --- |
| "I healed them." | "I held the field for healing." |
| "They are broken." | "They are shifting." |
| "I have the answers." | "Their field holds the map." |

## Personal Spiritual Leadership

To lead others in energy healing, you must walk your own inner path with honesty and humility.

- Cultivate your own daily realignment practice.
- Stay grounded in service, not power.
- Continue learning—especially about science, frequency, and consciousness evolution.

"If you want to find the secrets of the universe, think in terms of energy, frequency and vibration." — *Nikola Tesla*

Your personal vibration is part of every session. The more refined your field, the more refined your healing presence becomes.

# Appendices

## Where To Buy

- **Magnets & magnetic therapy supplies**: MagnetRX offers high-quality healing magnets and biomagnetic kits. MagnetRX
- **Magnetic bracelets, insoles, wraps**: Serenity2000 via Wellwise features magnetic therapy wearables for circulation & balance. Wellwise.ca
- **PEMF mats & full-body devices**: HigherDOSE's Infrared PEMF Pro Mat combines PEMF + far-infrared + gemstones. HigherDOSE
- **Magnetic & PEMF therapy devices wholesaler**: Relaxus offers a large selection of magnetic and PEMF therapy products. Relaxus Wholesale Canada
- **High-strength therapeutic magnets & accessories**: Auris (based in Europe) specializes in magnetotherapy products including strong neodymium options. Auris

*Tips for choosing quality tools*

- Look for **clear polarity labelling** (north/south) on magnets.
- Check **Gauss ratings** — start with lower strengths.
- For PEMF mats, verify the **frequency ranges**, materials, and certifications.

- Always read **contraindications** (pacemakers, pregnancy, tumors) before purchasing.
- Choose vendors with **good return policies**, clear specs, and educational info.

*Safety & ethics reminder*

These tools can be powerful, but they must be used wisely. Ensure your readers or clients know that **magnets, PEMF mats, and other field devices are not "magic cures"**, and they should be integrated with discernment, grounding, and healthy consent. Research remains mixed for some modalities.

## *Tool Summaries*

- Neodymium Healing Disc (North/South Polarity): Compact high-strength disc magnets clearly labelled North/South for targeted spot treatment of identified energy zones.
- Bipolar Magnetic Foot Insoles: Insoles embedded with alternating polarity magnets to support grounding and energetic circulation through the feet during daily activities.
- Magnetic Roller Wand: Hand-held roller that glides over meridians and muscular lines; useful for clearing congestion or stimulating energy flow.
- Infrared + PEMF Pro Mat: Full-body mat integrating pulsed electromagnetic fields (PEMF) with far-infrared warmth—ideal for broader field alignment in your realignment ritual.
- Bio-Well Aura & Biofield Scanner: Aura imaging device (GDV camera) which captures biofield patterns and helps practitioners map and monitor energetic changes.
- Healy Microcurrent & Frequency Wearable: Wearable device delivering tailored microcurrents

and frequency programs to support subtle energy balance and daily coherence.
- Crystal & Magnet Therapy Combo Kit: A kit combining carefully selected crystals and small magnets; aligns with sacred & esoteric modalities while anchoring Tesla-inspired magnetics.
- Tesla Coil Field Amplifier Unit: Specialty device that produces a low-level Tesla coil field, used alongside magnets for field-wide amplification; advanced practitioner tool.

## *1. Bio-Well / GDV Cameras – Measure aura and energy-field changes*

**How it works:** The Bio-Well uses Gas Discharge Visualization (GDV)-technology to measure subtle electrical discharges from the fingertips, capturing the "glow" or energy field around a person.

**Tesla-connection:** This aligns with Nikola Tesla's idea of matter and energy being fundamentally linked; measuring the field around the body makes the invisible visible.

**How to use:**

- Set up the camera in a stable, low-noise room.
- The person places their fingertips (or another specified position) on the sensor.
- Capture a scan and review the results; look for patterns of imbalance, stress, low energy.
- Use the scan to guide your Energeneic Mapping and tailor interventions (e.g., breath/tone/touch, magnetics).

**Notes:** Non-invasive, excellent for tracking progress before/after sessions. Useful as a visual feedback tool for clients.

## 2. Healy Device – Delivers micro-current / frequencies based on quantum sensors

**How it works:** The Healy is a wearable frequency-therapy device that uses micro-current and individualized frequency programs to support pain relief, relaxation, and energetic balance.

**Tesla-connection:** Tesla stressed frequency and vibration as keys to the universe. The Healy attempts to apply targeted frequencies to the human field, embodying that principle.

### How to use:

- Choose the program (e.g., pain relief, nervous system regulation, chakra balancing).
- Apply electrodes or wrist straps according to instructions.
- Run the cycle for the recommended duration (often 20-60 minutes).
- After the session, reflect on how you feel, scan your field or muscle-test to assess change.

**Notes:** This is a **supportive tool**, not a standalone cure. Monitor how the body responds.

## 3. NES Health System – Scans energetic distortions and delivers corrective infoceuticals

**How it works:** The NES Health system uses a scan of the subtle energy field, identifies "information imbalances", and applies corrective "infoceuticals" (energetic signatures) to restore coherence.

**Tesla-connection:** Tesla's work with electromagnetic fields underpins the concept of informational/energetic patterns influencing matter; NES tries to map and correct those patterns.

**How to use:**

- Perform field scan (via hardware/software).
- Analyze results to identify distortions or dysregulated zones.
- Apply the appropriate infoceutical program or device as directed (often a wearable or patch).
- Re-test after a defined period to monitor shift.

**Notes:** Integrated into practitioner protocols; can be more complex and requires training.

### 4. BEMER / PEMF Mats – Used for circulation, vitality, and energetic grounding

**How it works:** PEMF (Pulsed Electromagnetic Field) therapy uses carefully calibrated electromagnetic pulses to stimulate cell and tissue functions, enhance micro-circulation, and support the energetic field.

**Tesla-connection:** Tesla's work with high-voltage, low-current electromagnetic fields and resonance sets the precedent for devices that use pulses of electromagnetic energy for healing and recharging systems.

**How to use:**

- Lay the mat on a firm surface.
- Have the user lie on the mat (or place relevant body part) for a prescribed program.
- Duration may vary: 8-20 minutes for general support; longer for systemic resets.
- Post-session: ground the person (bare feet, simple breath), drink water, and follow up with a brief energetic scan.

**Notes:** For full-body alignment; excellent after mapping to correct widespread depletion or blockage.

# Sample ESR Protocol Script

*Energetic System Reset for Biofield Coherence & Tesla-Inspired Realignment*

Use this protocol to perform a full-body energetic reset using breath, tone, intention, mapping, and Tesla-inspired tools. Designed for practitioners or advanced clients.

1. Set the Space (1–2 min)

- **Environment:** Quiet room, no EMF distractions (turn off phones, WiFi if possible).
- **Tools Ready:** Pendulum or muscle testing tool, polarity-tested neodymium magnets, essential oils (if desired), magnetic wand or PEMF mat, tuning fork or sound bowl.
- **Intention:** "I open this space in service of healing, coherence, and realignment. I align with the highest frequency for this session."

2. Grounding & Breath Activation (2 min)

- Stand or sit barefoot.
- Inhale through the nose to a count of **4**, hold for **7**, exhale through the mouth for **8**.
- Repeat for 3 cycles.
- Imagine roots anchoring into the Earth. Feel magnetism rising into your field.

3. Energetic Mapping (5–7 min)

Use hands, pendulum, or muscle testing to identify:

- **Depletion:** Cool, collapsed zones.
- **Congestion:** Hot, dense, busy zones.
- **Blockage:** Dead zones, no signal.

**Voice cues:**

"Scan from crown to feet. Where does energy feel absent, chaotic, or frozen?"

**Mark findings on a body chart** or journal them briefly.

4. Emotional Inquiry Prompt (2–3 min)

Ask the body or the client:

- "What am I not expressing here?"
- "What is this energy trying to tell me?"
- "What frequency is stuck here?"

Let the answer rise. Don't force. Simply notice.

5. Reset Sequence: Breath – Tone – Touch (5 min)

- **Breath:** Do **Vertical Box Breathing**—inhale up the spine (4 sec), hold (4 sec), exhale down the spine (4 sec), hold (4 sec). Repeat 4x.
- **Tone:** Let the client hum on the exhale. Let the tone match the area of congestion.
- **Touch:** Gently tap K27 points, heart center, and sacral chakra. Use two fingers, tap rhythmically.

6. Magnetic or Frequency Intervention (Optional – 5–10 min)

Choose based on field distortion:

- **Neodymium Disc** (low-gauss): Place near congested areas (not over heart, brain, or if contraindicated).
- **Magnetic Wand:** Roll from crown to soles in spiraling motion (clockwise).

- **PEMF Mat:** Have client lie on the mat for 8–15 min.
- **Healy/NES/Infoceutical Drops:** If available, apply per protocol for client's field needs.

7. Realignment Ritual (2–3 min)

- State intention clearly:

  "I now choose coherence, clarity, and flow. I align all systems with my highest blueprint."

- Optional:
  - Diffuse oils like frankincense or pine.
  - Ring a bell, chime, or fork at crown, heart, and root.
  - Place hands in prayer pose over heart.

8. Closing Reflection

- Ask the client: "What do you notice now?"
- Note changes in temperature, breath, clarity, posture, or emotion.

## Encouragement:

Integration may continue for 24–72 hours.
Drink water.
Walk in nature.
Journal your insights.

# Bibliography

*For Bioenergetics: The Energeneic Practitioner – A Modern Guide to Healing the Energy Body Through Touch, Frequency & Subtle Sensing*

Core Books & Foundational Texts

- Thie, John & Thie, Matthew. *Touch for Health: The Complete Edition*. DeVorss & Company, 2005.
- Oschman, James L. *Energy Medicine: The Scientific Basis*. Elsevier, 2000.
- Gerber, Richard. *Vibrational Medicine: The #1 Handbook of Subtle-Energy Therapies*. Bear & Company, 2001.
- Becker, Robert O. & Selden, Gary. *The Body Electric: Electromagnetism and the Foundation of Life*. William Morrow, 1985.
- Shealy, C. Norman. *Energy Medicine: Practical Applications and Scientific Proof*. Are Press, 2000.
- Pert, Candace B. *Molecules of Emotion: The Science Behind Mind-Body Medicine*. Scribner, 1997.

Scientific and Academic References

- Rubik, Beverly et al. "Biofield Science: Current Physics Perspectives." *Global Advances in Health and Medicine*, 2015.
- National Institutes of Health (NIH) / National Center for Complementary and Integrative Health (NCCIH). *Biofield Therapies: Summary of Evidence* – nccih.nih.gov.
- Popp, Fritz-Albert. *Biophotonen: Das Licht in unseren Zellen*. Munich: Droemer Knaur, 2002.

TESLA'S BIOENERGETICS BLUEPRINT | 133

- Bohm, David. *Wholeness and the Implicate Order.* Routledge, 1980.
- Lipton, Bruce H. *The Biology of Belief: Unleashing the Power of Consciousness, Matter & Miracles.* Hay House, 2005.

## Modalities & Techniques

- Dennison, Paul E. & Dennison, Gail E. *Brain Gym®: Teacher's Edition.* Edu-Kinesthetics, Inc., 2010.
- Eden, Donna. *Energy Medicine: Balancing Your Body's Energies for Optimal Health, Joy, and Vitality.* TarcherPerigee, 2008.
- Stone, Randolph. *Polarity Therapy: The Complete Collected Works.* CRCS Publications, 1994.
- Mein, Carla. *Color and Sound Healing.* Transformation Publishing, 1995.
- Gach, Michael Reed. *Acupressure's Potent Points: A Guide to Self-Care for Common Ailments.* Bantam, 1990.

## Complementary Systems Referenced

- Traditional Chinese Medicine theory (Five Elements, Meridians, Yin/Yang)
- Vedic Chakra System (Root to Crown energy centers)
- Wilhelm Reich & Orgone Energy concepts:
    - Reich, Wilhelm. *The Function of the Orgasm.* Farrar, Straus and Giroux, 1973.
    - DeMeo, James. *The Orgone Accumulator Handbook.* Natural Energy Works, 2010.

## Aromatherapy and Frequency

- Worwood, Valerie Ann. *The Fragrant Mind.* New World Library, 1995.

- Schnaubelt, Kurt. *Medical Aromatherapy: Healing with Essential Oils.* Frog Ltd., 1999.
- Goldman, Jonathan & Goldman, Andi. *The Humming Effect: Sound Healing for Health and Happiness.* Healing Arts Press, 2017.
- Tiller, William A. *Science and Human Transformation.* Pavior Publishing, 1997.

Additional Resources

- National Center for Complementary and Integrative Health (NCCIH) – https://nccih.nih.gov
- International Kinesiology College – https://www.ikc-info.org
- Touch for Health Kinesiology Association – https://www.touchforhealth.us

**Note to Reader:**
This list is not exhaustive, but it includes the pioneers and thinkers whose contributions paved the way for the Quick Fix method. Exploring these resources will deepen your appreciation of the body's innate intelligence and the many traditions that honor its ability to heal.

# Message from the Author

*D*ear Readers,

When I first began this journey into energy healing over two decades ago, I never imagined it would lead me to explore the profound legacy of Nikola Tesla, the unseen forces of the human energy field, and the astonishing healing technologies now emerging from the fusion of ancient wisdom and modern science.

This book is not simply a manual or a catalogue of tools—it is a bridge. A bridge between worlds: the scientific and the spiritual, the electromagnetic and the intuitive, the remembered and the yet-to-be-revealed. Each technique, protocol, and insight included here was chosen not just for its effectiveness, but for its resonance with a new kind of healer—one who leads with integrity, aligns with natural law, and trusts the body's deep intelligence to restore itself.

I believe we are in a renaissance—a time when healing is returning to its rightful place as both an art and a science. You, dear reader, are part of that awakening. Whether you are just beginning to explore energetic tools or you've been working in this field for years, my hope is that this book meets you exactly where you are—and invites you into deeper curiosity, grounded experimentation, and soul-led service.

Thank you for being here. Thank you for choosing to become a Tesla-style healer—not just by what you know, but by how you live and serve. The future of healing is in our hands, our hearts, and our frequencies.

With deep respect and gratitude,
**Dr. Constance Santego**

# About the Author

**D**r. Constance Santego, Ph.D., DNM, is a pioneering force in the fields of energy medicine, vibrational healing, and holistic wellness education. With a background that bridges both ancient healing traditions and cutting-edge technologies, Dr. Santego is known for her ability to blend intuitive wisdom with scientific innovation.

She is the founder of multiple wellness and educational platforms, where she empowers students, authors, and healers around the world to unlock their highest potential. A Grand Reiki Master and Natural Medicine Doctor with over 25 years of experience, she has written more than 70 books on topics ranging from Reiki and energy healing to personal transformation, intuitive development, and spiritual fiction.

In addition to her writings, Dr. Santego has trained thousands of students in person and online, guiding them in the practical use of modalities such as Reiki, muscle testing, bioenergetics, and now—Tesla-style frequency healing. Her work is rooted in the belief that healing is not only possible—it is inevitable when we align with the natural laws of energy, intention, and spiritual coherence.

A passionate speaker, teacher, and creator, Dr. Santego's mission is to raise global consciousness through education, empowerment, and energetic mastery.

She lives in beautiful British Columbia, Canada, where she continues to write, teach, and develop transformative healing systems for the modern world.

# Discover More

**Embark on an Adventure with "Ikona – Discover Your Inner Genie"**

Dive deeper into the world of empowerment and self-discovery with a range of offerings designed to inspire and transform. Explore the full spectrum of Constance Santego's motivational products, personalized coaching sessions, spiritual retreats, engaging live events, and enriching educational programs.

**Connect, Learn, and Grow:**

- Website: Journey further into our resources and offerings at www.ConstanceSantego.ca.
- Instagram: Join our community @Constance_Santego for daily inspiration and insights.
- Facebook: Stay updated with the latest events and connect with like-minded individuals on Constance Santego's Facebook Page.
- YouTube: Subscribe to Constance Santego's YouTube Channel for free resources, meditations, and more to guide you on your path to self-improvement.

Your journey toward personal growth and enlightenment is just a click away. Discover the tools and support you need to unlock your potential and manifest your dreams.

www.ingramcontent.com/pod-product-compliance
Lightning Source LLC
Chambersburg PA
CBHW051201120626
46547CB00012B/1150